RELEASING THE FEAR
and
Walking in Faith

RANELLI WILLIAMS

LOVE CLONES
publishing

Love Clones Publishing
www.lcpublishing.net

Printed in the United States of America

First Printing, 2014

ISBN: 978-0692711514

Publishers:
Love Clones Publishing
Dallas, TX 75025
www.lcpublishing.net

DEDICATION

This book is for anyone who hopes to move beyond fear and take the incredible walk of faith into God's greatness. My prayer is that it will empower its readers to achieve something exceptional in their lives.

I want to thank God for calling me to this mission to not only help His people release their fears and walk in faith, but also to strengthen my own faith.

I dedicate this book to my two sons, Joeraan and Jaevaan. You are my inspiration. Never allow fear to hold you back from doing great exploits for God.

ACKNOWLEDGMENTS

I thank my husband, Eric Williams, for holding it together and believing in me as I spent hours in writing. You are an awesome man of God and I love you.

I want to thank my mom, Elizabeth Lindsey, for your support and for instilling Christian values in me and for bringing me up in the church where I learned so many scriptures that just came back to memory as I penned my thoughts. You have also been an inspiring example of true work ethic. You are a true blessing indeed!

My dad, Randolph Riley, thank you for your support and for your entrepreneurial drive, which I undoubtedly adopted from you.

Carlene Charlemagne-Eddings, you birthed this ministry in me by pushing me beyond my fears, I thank you.

Denise Mock, your mentorship has moved me out of my comfort zone and into a whole new world of fabulous connections and invaluable Christian relationships.

Candace Ford, thank you for working with me through the original process of writing. Your patience and support have been instrumental in getting this done.

Pastor Livingstone Aaron, I truly appreciate your spiritual guidance and advice during this writing assignment and in general.

Aprille Franks-Hunt, God put you in my life for such a time as this. Your wisdom and drive to see others succeed is bar none. Thank you for being a great coach. You helped to birth this fire in me to serve with excellence and I am forever grateful.

Tamika Simms and my sister, Chezline Riley, thank you for being great editors. I appreciate you.

Lastly, to all 23 of the ladies who courageously shared their testimonies in this book, I am humbled that you opened up your hearts to share with the readers what God has done in your life through faith. May your seed of openness and willingness to share, bring you great harvest.

Endorsements

The more I venture in my own journey as a woman, a leader, and a philanthropist, I am reminded that releasing my perceived fear and standing strong in my faith and actions is imperative to my growth. In Releasing the Fear & Walking in Faith, I am reminded on so many occasions that I am on the right track. Ranelli did an amazing job giving the reader tangible resources and stories that mirror real life in so many ways! This book should be in every spiritual community to help inspire and motivate others to walk in their full authentic purpose.

Aprille Franks-Hunt
Founder & CEO of Women Recharged

In this seminal work, Ranelli Williams explores the anatomy of faith and its transcendent power over fear, which is deemed an "undercurrent, subtle and unassuming." She underpins her thesis of redemption from fear not just by theory and enthusiastic exhortation, but by exemplars drawn both from scripture and the acts of living apostles and witnesses. She demonstrates the virtues of faith and perseverance not just by reference to Job and Jabez, but to Atarah and Lisa next door, along with the likes of R. H. Macy and Michael Jordan of global fame. It was faith that came to their rescue when they had cause to falter and faint with fear.

Williams does not offer a facile solution to fear which is perceived as a natural part of being human. Recognizing the "curved balls" which life throws at people, she writes with a realistic concept of fear and the negativity that has to be fought through faith, building brick upon brick. It is an empowering text with practical guidelines. What can be termed her dictum of faith and action: "You have to dream to Do," is fascinating and insightful.

This book, at once instructive and inspirational, is a compelling guide to persons of all faiths within the Christian universe and even to those outside who want to be made whole. While the volume is rooted in biblical lore and a sensible theology, the author's wide reading adds a strong cognitive element, which makes the work doubly appealing to all class and condition.

I am pleased to endorse this potential best seller in a world adrift, thronged by problems that must be addressed by the kind of faith that casts out fear.

Sir Dr. Howard A. Fergus
Formerly, Professor, University of the West Indies
(Montserrat, West Indies)

This book by Ranelli Williams brings hope for those who have been imprisoned in fear. It speaks to an experience which all persons have had at some time, that of being fearful. It offers a clear guide by which anyone can accomplish the task of breaking loose of this shackle. It speaks of the freedom that comes through faith, prayer, meditation, journaling and much more. The testimonials are so human, the writing is clear and the mind is invigorated by each chapter read. This compelling book is a salve to all who must face these times and it invigorates, while inviting all to walk in faith.

H. Hugh Maynard-Reid,
Director Of Pastoral Care Service
North Brooklyn Health Network

TABLE OF CONTENTS

PREFACE

The most repeated command in the Bible is "Do Not Fear" or "Fear Not." God in His wisdom knew that fear would be a stronghold in the lives of His children. God wants fear exposed. He wants His people to stop believing the lie of fear and start trusting in Him. He wants us to put our full dependence in Him. Are you ready to stop being afraid and start living? If your answer is yes, then let's journey together as we release the fear and walk in faith.

Walking in faith looks something like this: Your eyes are fixed on God. You do not allow the cares of this world to distract your focus. As a matter of fact, because of those cares, your focus becomes more intent. Nothing or no one intimidates you. You are not moved by the negative things in your life or around you. Your arms are stretched toward heaven. Your posture is strong. Your chin is up and head held high. Your shoulders leaned back and your chest out. You are strong, courageous and confident. Though you cannot see the light, you pray for God to guide you in the right direction as you start to move. There are stumbling blocks in your way and you get tired at times but you keep on moving. In your moving forward, things begin to get clearer, you start seeing what could be the light. As you journey on, you realize, yes, it is the light and you quicken your steps and start moving closer and closer and closer until alas! what you have been believing for is now perfectly clear.

Journey on. Take small steps if you must, but step. Don't let fear hold you back. Walk in faith!

A Special Message To My Readers

Dear Friend,

Imagine this! Two weeks and two days after launching the original edition of this book, I received a call from my job notifying me that they no longer needed my services. I will never compare myself to Job but I felt like God gave the enemy permission to attack because He knew I just went through the process of scribing what the walk of faith looks like. It was now my opportunity to exercise the faith I wrote about in my book.

I thought I was ready and knew it was the opportunity for me to jump into full-time entrepreneurship, and boy has it been a ride. Nothing went as planned. My network marketing business that was starting to take off again and that I was ready to fully thrust myself into, experienced some major changes that shook the company at its core. Having considered this home for the previous four years, taking a break was the last thing I wanted to do but after several promptings from the Holy Spirit, it was evident that focusing on my personal business with my husband needed to be top priority.

However, even when I felt as if I was pouring everything into my business, ERJ Services, funds were not flowing in according to plan. The brook was drying up and fear started to kick in. There were moments of worry and panic to the point that it became difficult to talk to God. Yes, I allowed myself to go there. Some friends even began pulling away and the journey was becoming quite lonely. Onlookers would cheer from a distance but without true support from most. Things were looking grim, at least through my eyes. I was learning and growing but the financial reality was clouding my viewpoint.

I began doubting my abilities and purpose. How could I help people with their finances when my own recovery process was starting to go in the wrong direction? My actions began to embrace this mindset. I started and stopped a gratitude jar before the first month was over. I watched the movie War Room and couldn't muster up what it took to create my own war room, although I needed it. On the outside things appeared great; except for those times I was told I looked "tired". This went on until I truly learned what it meant to surrender.

The day I made a desperate cry, God showed up. Well, He was there all along but I was blinded by concern. However, His messages to me this day were so clear, the path became plain. And the path was simply to trust Him.

The specific messages I got that day which I want to share with you as encouragement were:

1. I am in control.
2. Your hard work will be rewarded.
3. Your test will be your testimony.

4.   Your path to success is like a rollercoaster ride. Embrace the journey.

5.   Speak life into your situation.

6.   Daily declare and decree the state(s) you are looking to acquire.

7.   You are empowered because I AM.

8.   Don't grow weary as you wait. I know exactly what I am doing.

9.   You already have the formula: hard work, determination, and discipline. Keep living it.

10.   Live in gratitude.

With these profound messages coming to me in one day, I released the fear, documented this experience and began the journey of walking in faith. This is my testimony today:

- I am Ranelli Williams.
- I am a child of THE King.
- I am fearfully and wonderfully made.
- I am royalty.
- I deserve the best.
- I live an abundant life.
- I am a respected Certified Public Accountant.
- I am a wealth activation strategist.
- I help my clients gain clarity with their financial plan.
- I build generational wealth God's way.
- I represent the I AM.
- I live in gratitude.

- I am a faith and legacy building catalyst.

As a faith and legacy building catalyst and CEO of The Legacy Builders Network, I am called to a higher standard. I am called not just to be, do, and have more for myself. I am called to be more than just the Chief Family Visionary (coined from my accountability partner Donna Hicks-Izzard), working towards changing my family's financial history and educating my boys on building generational wealth. I am also called to be a voice, educating those I serve to choose faith and walk in the value that they are and that they bring to the table as children of God called to a higher purpose. We will no longer cower in fear! We will step up together in passion and purpose.

Best,
Ranelli Williams

WRITE THROUGH THE FEAR

Scripture:
"Fear ye not, neither be afraid: have not I told thee from that time, and have declared it? ye are even my witnesses. Is there a God beside me? yea, there is no God; I know not any." Isaiah 44:8

Lesson

Spiritual gifts are given to each of God's children, you being one of them. Here's what the scriptures say in 1 Corinthians 12:7-11. "Now to each one the manifestation of the Spirit is given for the common good. To one there is given through the Spirit a message of wisdom, to another a message of knowledge by means of the same Spirit, to another faith by the same Spirit, to another gifts of healing by that one Spirit, to another miraculous powers, to another prophecy, to another distinguishing between spirits, to another speaking in different kinds of tongues, and to still another the interpretation of tongues. All these are the work of one and the same Spirit, and he distributes them to each one, just as he determines."

For a while I struggled with what my spiritual gifts were. I knew I was blessed with a voice to sing but I never felt the calling to take my singing beyond my ministry in church. However, I always felt that God had great plans for me to minister to His people in a big way but I could never pinpoint how. So when I was called to write a book, I knew that this could potentially allow me to reach a wide audience, but since I never considered myself to be a writer, I started to fear and doubt. My strong subjects in school were Math, Business and Accounting. Thus, when the Lord placed it in my heart to start a ministry and write a book, in an area where I myself had struggle, my initial response was, I cannot do that.

This was definitely a test for me. I certainly had no confidence in myself. That's not my calling Lord, I said. I was telling the Lord what my calling was. What a joke! The God of the universe who sees the end from the beginning, I was refusing to follow His plan. You see how crazy that is? Corrie ten Boom said it best, "Never be afraid to trust an unknown future to a known God."

Through Habakkuk 2:2, God made it clear to me that I should write the vision and make it plain, so those who read it might run with it. And so in faith, I set out on this writing journey on a subject that God wanted to use to teach me. God knew that I needed to stop fearing and start "faithing". This journey has been amazingly eye opening for me as I learned through scripture to put my trust in God in all things. I say like David, "My heart is overflowing with a good theme; I write my composition concerning the King; my tongue is the pen of a ready writer" (Psalm 45:1,

NKJV).

How about you? Do you feel called to write? Even if you don't feel called right now or you are not sure, start journaling today. Every one of us has a story to tell or a message to impart. For some of you the story will be told through your hospitality, or maybe through song, or maybe through your business, and for some of you it will be through your writing. Do not tell God what you can and cannot do. Philippians 4:13 says, "I can do ALL things through Christ who gives me strength." God does not call the equipped but rather He equips those whom He calls. Just learn to say yes Lord and certainly don't be afraid to bloom where you are planted.

Prayer

Father, thank You for Your confidence in me, especially when I do not have confidence in myself. God, I am nothing without You, but with You I can do the impossible. You know what's best for me Lord, so please Help me to trust You and follow the path You are leading. I am ready to do Your will because I can never go wrong with You as my guide. Prepare my heart and my mind for whatever You ask me to do. In Jesus' name. Amen!

Testimony – Jennifer Fontanilla

Before I was 30, I was successful as a senior graphic designer working on various projects for the entertainment and video game industry. I had accumulated wealth, owned multiple properties in southern California and possessed this mentality that I was going somewhere.

That somewhere went nowhere in a heartbeat after the market crashed and along with the financial crisis, I experienced my own marital crash. Financial pressures took a stronghold over us, infidelity crept in and caused the demise of our "happily ever after". I lost confidence in anything I was doing and fear sank in. I wanted to give up and become complacent.

As if this wasn't hard enough, the following year I discovered I was going to be a mother. It was unexpected and of course, in my opinion, the most inconvenient timing. I couldn't imagine the possibility of rebuilding my life and business at this point. Had it not been for the supportive help of my parents, I would have found myself homeless or suicidal. My healthy baby boy was born and he was given all the love and attention he deserved. With worry set aside, I now had to regain focus on my life.

Completely unplanned, I decided to do some work at a local Starbucks. As usual, all the tables and chairs were occupied except for one spot at a large table. I squeezed myself onto the bench and it happened that the woman sitting next to me was a friend I had met at this same place more than a year ago. We quickly caught up and she blessed me with a devotional by Beth Moore. I thought to myself, "How am I going to stay diligent and write in this thing for 70 days straight?!" I gracefully accepted the gift, half excited and half scared. I didn't know what to expect.

I was already lost, confused and afraid my life was going nowhere so what did I have to lose? For the first day, I sparingly wrote answers just to fill in the blank lines, but I knew I needed to put my heart into it. It wouldn't be another week until I would write for Day 2. Slowly, but surely, it became easier and easier and I found myself loving the time I would spend immersed in God's word and the lesson for the day. My excitement for spending my quiet mornings with Him is what got me out of bed before the sun came up. For the first time, I realized how powerful writing out my thoughts were. Each day I would praise Him, repent, acknowledge Him, pray for others, ask for what I needed and then end it with asking Him to equip me.

I began to see God in a different light. I was able to let go of certain fears and anxiety, especially that of my future. The more I learned He is in control, it gave me hope that I didn't need to worry and that He would provide. I relearned I was a child of the most-high God and I would receive the inheritance He has promised (Galatians 4: 6-7). All the things I lost no longer carried importance. Others' opinions of me or what I had failed at faded into the background. The only thing that mattered was that I was God's building project, His handiwork, created in Christ to do His work (Ephesians 2:10).

God's timing is always perfect and it was no coincidence this book was placed in my hands this day. Although I have always prayed and have known God, this time it was different, with a pen in my hand as I wrote my thoughts and fears, and acknowledged I needed Him each and every day. I am reminded I was chosen to share in God's Heavenly calling. When I place my hope in this, my fear of the future fades away. The peace and calmness that it has given me is indescribable and lets me know it could only come from my God above.

Jennifer Fontanilla
www.jenniferfontanilla.com
jennifer.fontanilla@gmail.com

Action Plan
Start a journal. Write in your journal daily and allow the Spirit to lead.

_____

_____

_____

_____

_____

ACT THROUGH THE FEAR

Scripture

"But now, this is what the LORD says-- he who created you, Jacob, he who formed you, Israel: "Do not fear, for I have redeemed you; I have summoned you by name; you are mine." Isaiah 43:1

Lesson

Procrastination is defined as putting things off as long as you can and is nothing more than the fear of taking action. Yes, you procrastinate when you are afraid of moving beyond thinking into doing. You are afraid to fail. You do not want the world and people around you to see your shortcomings. You are worried you won't do it right. I know many of us have been raised to believe mistakes and failure are bad and that if you fail you'll be rejected. The reality is, no one wants to be rebuffed or have people think badly of them. However, founding your self-worth on what others think of you will cause fear and prevent you from moving forward. Here is my suggestion. Consider establishing your self-worth on what God thinks of you. Are you aware that He thinks the world of you? He really does. Read again what He says in our scripture passage, Isaiah 43:1.

It's time to take action. Remember God said in 2 Corinthians 12:9, *"...my strength is made perfect in your weakness...*" Do not wait for the perfect time because this time will never come. God intends for you to step out on faith and take action. He expects you to do this in spite of everything that's happening inside of and around you. While you have very little control on what is happening around you, you certainly have control of what is happening on the inside. Through the grace of God and the power He has given to you through His son Jesus Christ and the Holy Spirit, your negative thoughts can become positive. You are a force to be reckoned with once God is on your side. All you have to do is accept that He is always with you. He said in Matthew 28:20, *"I am with you always even unto the end of the world".*

Ok, so now you've got it. God is on your side and expects you to take action. How do you do that?

It is simple. You really have to muster up the guts and do it. One of my favorite motivational speakers, Les Brown, in his "No Guts, No Glory" speech said, *"Hard times have not come to stay. They have come to pass. Have faith and patience and engage in consistent action. Faith takes guts and without guts, there is no glory."* Always remember, your dream and the beautiful picture you envision at the end of the journey will not happen automatically. You have to take action. You have to DO your dream.

After you get to work, you must seek out support. One of the leading obstacles that prevent people from taking action is their thinking they have to do it on their own. Ezra 10:4 (NIV) says "*Rise up; this matter is in your hands. We will support you, so take courage and do it.*" You can and should always reach out to others for help. Don't worry if you do not get the support from the people directly around you. The important thing is that you get it from somewhere and you never forget God is always there by your side.

Seek out mentors and coaches. Once you get the right individuals in your corner, they will be the best earthly support systems you can ask for. Edmund Lee says it best, *"Surround yourself with the dreamers and the doers, the believers and thinkers, but most of all, surround yourself with those who see the greatness within you, even when you don't see it yourself."*

Lastly, *"What good is it, my brothers and sisters, if someone claims to have faith but has no deeds? Can such faith save them? Suppose a brother or a sister is without clothes and daily food. If one of you says to them, "Go in peace; keep warm and well fed," but does nothing about their physical needs, what good is it? In the same way, faith by itself, if it is not accompanied by action, is dead"* (James 2:14-17, NIV). When you refuse to take action, you are refusing to provide much needed help, encouragement, and support to someone else. Do not deny yourself or others the greatness inside of you.

Mark Batterson says, *"When everything is said and done, God won't say, 'Well SAID, good and faithful servant.' He won't say, 'Well THOUGHT, well PLANNED, or even, well PRAYED.' There is only one commendation He will give: 'Well DONE, good and faithful servant.'"* Make a move. Act through the fear. God will be your guide.

Prayer

Father, I thank You for exposing procrastination for what it is. Help me to move beyond the fear of procrastination into action. Help me to always remember that I am Yours and You have called me by name. Lord, I am tired of how I have allowed my fears to hold me back and I am ready to take action and move forward, but I cannot do it on my own. Help me first to rely on You and then I pray that You would place the right Christian support system in my life. I thank You for calling me on this mission in life to bless others and build up Your Kingdom. I want to do Your will. I declare by the power of the Holy Spirit and through the strength of Your Son Jesus Christ, I will step out in faith and take action to further Your cause. In Jesus' name. Amen!

Testimony – Xkizin Wright

I continued to get better with acting through fear, but this was not always the case. I had to learn how not to let the fear of rejection stop me from living and moving into my passion. When I was growing up, I always knew I wanted to help others. I was willing to try anything because I was open-minded and had an entrepreneurial spirit. I thought the best way to combine my love of helping others and entrepreneurship was through selling life insurance. It appeared to be a perfect combination. The commissions were lucrative and it helped people at an emotional time in their lives. However, I was ill prepared for the level of rejection I would encounter and every "No" magnified my fear.

I was harboring some deep-seated fear and pain of rejection due to an incident that happened in my youth. Granted, I became good at coping with those feelings as I became older, but my foray into the world of selling insurance, quickly and brutally brought those feelings to the surface. It became clear that the fear of facing the pain of rejection was hindering my ability to be successful. With my sincere desire to help others release their past hurts so they can live the life they desire, I knew this had to be addressed. It became obvious that I must be a model worth copying.

In May 2014 while volunteering with an organization that serves entrepreneurs and CEO's who made six and seven figures annually, I had my "aha" moment. During an activity where the participants were working on their next quarter goals, one of the individuals started to cry. She stated that this could not be done. She felt as if she could not do it and it was too hard. It was the beginning of many situations where I realized I was not alone. Furthermore, possessing a healthy level of fear is okay, what matters is what you do with it. With my personal experience plus my exposure to other entrepreneurs that have been hindered by fear, it became clear that my calling was in the service as an Entrepreneur Therapist.

I wanted to start working towards my purpose but the fear and lack of faith was still there. I knew something had to change. I began to work on increasing my faith in my abilities, so it would override my fear. During this process, I was offered an opportunity to participate in a group-coaching program where I learned how to create content. I was creating a program to help entrepreneurs overcome mental hurdles that were holding them back from achieving success. As I completed the creation of my course, my coach challenged me to do a pre-launch of my program. Yikes! The rush of fear was overwhelming. I was beyond terrified! The aforementioned fear of rejection combined with negative self-talk almost stopped me in my tracks.

However, during the program I realized my purpose and passion is not for me but for the individuals I am meant to serve. This is when I realized I am a vessel created to accomplish what was given to me, so my fear is irrelevant. After this slap in the face, I realized I needed to snap out of it. I went ahead and did a pre-launch of my product regardless of my fear and even though I felt I was not 100% prepared. After the pre-launch, I learned a powerful lesson about dealing with fear and how to overcome it. When I took the emphasis off me and began to focus on who I am serving, I became unstoppable in the level of service and energy I give to see others succeed. Lastly, I realized fear is a natural part of being human. Courage is the ability to take action in spite of it. Your act of bravery could be all the inspiration someone needs to live his or her dreams. #Doitscared

Xkizin Wright
www.xkizinwright.com
xkizinwright@gmail.com

Action Plan

1. Answer the following questions:
   a. What fear have you been clinging to?
   b. How does this fear hold you back in life?
   c. How has this fear helped you in the past and how does this fear help you now?
   d. What would be your payoff for eliminating this fear?

2. Remind yourself of what you learned in the lesson above. Now develop a plan of action.

_____

_____

_____

_____

_____

_____

_____

_____

_____

_____

_____

_____

_____

_____

_____

_____

_____

_____

_____

_____

_____

_____

BELIEVE ABOVE THE FEAR

Scripture
"After these things the word of the Lord came unto Abram in a vision, saying, Fear not, Abram: I am your shield, and your exceeding great reward."
Genesis 15:1

Lesson I

When Abram (whose name was not yet changed to Abraham) learned his nephew Lot was taken captive when Sodom and Gomorrah were overtaken, He gathered his troops and marched in and rescued Lot, his people and their possessions. Abram showed no fear. He boldly went on the rescue mission for his nephew.

Follow Abram's example. Don't ever let fear hold you back from doing what you know is right. Have you ever seen someone, a man, woman, boy, or girl in an abusive situation? Yet you refused to do anything about it for fear of retaliation or because you have convinced yourself that it is none of your business? Well, it is your business. You are your brother's (and sister's) keeper. Don't get me wrong. I am aware that this could be a tricky situation so don't treat it lightly. All I am saying is don't turn a blind eye. Encourage the victim to seek professional help and support in any way you can.

Abram could have chosen to turn the other way for fear that he and his army were not powerful enough to defeat Kedorlaomer and the kings allied with him. Abram trusted God. You are called to be like Abram. *"The Lord is my light and my salvation, whom shall I fear. The Lord is the strength of my life, of whom shall I be afraid. When the wicked, even my enemies and my foes, came upon me to eat up my flesh, they stumbled and fell. Though an host should encamp against me, my heart shall not fear; though war should rise against me, in this will I be confident"* *(Psalm 27:1-3).* It is important that you develop the same confidence Abram had. Abram put the well being of his nephew in front of his own. Don't let fear stop you from doing a good deed and saving someone from the enemy. Be bold in your belief, actions, and walk with God.

Lesson II

Sometimes, even when we experience how God has worked with and in us, and led us through difficult situations in our life, we still tend to allow our current situations to trip us. Although Abram had just witnessed God's guidance and His protective hand as he rescued Lot, he still became saddened and doubted God regarding being childless and not having an heir to his estate. However, he quickly erased his doubt and sadness once he heard the word of the Lord, in a vision. Genesis 15:1-5 states, *"Do not be afraid Abram. I will shield you and will reward you exceedingly. A son who is your own flesh and blood will be your heir.... Your offspring shall be as much as the stars in the sky."* These words were comforting to Abram. He immediately believed God. Because of his belief, he received exactly what God promised.

What seemingly impossible situation are you going through? Have you taken the time to listen to the still small voice of your Savior? What is He saying to you regarding this situation? Pause. Listen. God is speaking. When we pause to listen, we hear God's voice, and He speaks clearly. Trust Him. Believe what He tells you.

Remember what He has done for you in the past and the promises He has made. The same provisions given to Abram are given to us as his seed. God promised to reward us. Claim it. Be bold in your mission. Be intentional in your belief. Refuse to be discouraged when it seems as if everything around you is falling apart. Choose to believe and watch God work out every little detail!

Prayer

Lord, I thank You for Your Word. I thank You Father that You care for Your people today, just as You cared for Abram. Father, You promised Abram that You would be his shield, and that You would reward him greatly. Thank You for making me Abraham's seed. Thank You that the same instructions and promises You gave Abram, You gave to me. Thank You that I am able to experience the manifestation of Your promises. You told us in Your word that if we believe, we would receive whatever we asked for in prayer (Matthew 21:22). You have proven time and again Your word is true and that whatever You say You will do, You will. So Father, today I choose to believe. I choose to have faith in You. Lord, I will no longer allow fear to have power over me. I rejoice in this freedom. In Jesus' name. Amen!

Testimony – Necie Black

Change is a scary process, but positive change adds value to our life that it's worth pushing through the challenges. Not to mention the value it adds to our confidence. Think about it - how many times have you found yourself backed into a corner, feeling as if you had no choice. You needed to make a decision but were afraid of what may come afterwards. You were afraid things wouldn't turn out the way you wanted. Then when you made your decision you felt an overwhelming sense of relief; the anxiety passed and you wondered, *"Why in the world was I so afraid?"*

I am raising both hands because many times this was me! I contemplated and over thought stuff to death. I called it analyzing when in reality it was an element of fear. I made so many bad decisions in my life that I questioned my ability to make a good one. After having a child at 16 years of age, I worked hard to make a life for my daughter and I. During the process, I found myself attracted to the wrong type of men, sacrificing my dignity for anyone who paid attention to me.

Yes, I had a great career and made a decent income to care for my kids. Yet when it came to matters of the heart, I was suffering. When it came to standing up for who I was, I was silent, and when it came to imagining life beyond my circumstances, I had no vision. The result was settling into relationships that were not good for me, believing I couldn't do any better. It meant keeping my head down, paying the bills, taking care of the kids and working for them to have a better life. Not realizing that I could have a better life too – if I wanted it, and I did.

My shift came when I divorced my second husband. I was finally alone; no relationship, no man, and no desire for one. It was me and God. I spent time really looking over my life; what I had done, what I left undone, and all I really wanted to do. For the first time in my life I saw the woman I had become and I wasn't happy with her. I prayed and cried a lot, and spent weeks figuring out what to do next. I took responsibility for my past actions and stopped making excuses for where I was in life. I learned to trust God and myself again and believe there was more for me. I was terribly afraid of the future, so trusting didn't come easy for me.

I had to start somewhere, here's where it all began:

- I changed my perspective and focused on what I did right; then built my next step on that.
- I looked at the poor choices and the lessons in those mistakes. I changed my thinking and did things differently when those "situations" came around again – and they did.
- I began trusting my instinct; trusting that God prepared me for whatever walking in my purpose called for next.
- I gave myself grace when things didn't turn out as planned. Trusting I did my best and continued to move forward.
- I refused to listen to negativity – in fact, I separated myself from it. That meant loving some people from a distance.
- I changed my life one baby step at a time; even stumbling and falling forward. I began to celebrate each and every win along the way.

As my confidence grew, so did my decision making ability. I stopped limiting myself to things I was comfortable doing and ventured outside of the comfortable and familiar box. Of course we are always a work in process, so I encourage you to keep your eyes and heart focused on your now and future –

whatever change is for you. Envision your future and how living the life you want will make you feel. Let nothing and no one stand in the way of your dreams. You've got this and you are ready. Stay faithful, consistent, and intentional and push through to the other side of fear!

Necie Black
www.necieblack.com
necieblack62@gmail.com

Action Plan

Pen your understanding of the lesson and the area of your life you are choosing to surrender to God today, knowing and believing He will hear and answer your prayer if you believe. As you journal your thoughts, read and meditate on James 1:6, "*But when you ask, you must believe and not doubt, because the one who doubts is like a wave of the sea, blown and tossed by the wind.*"

_____

_____

_____

_____

_____

_____

_____

BUILD AROUND THE FEAR

Scripture

"For I am the LORD your God who takes hold of your right hand and says to you, Do not fear; I will help you." Isaiah 41:13

Lesson

Although God has promised He will help us, He still expects us to do the work. Understand He did not say He would do it for you, He said He would help you. One of the greatest mistakes you and I make is waiting for a "door of opportunity" to open for us. The reality is we were created to build the doors of opportunity. Build what's in your heart. Until you build, your boundaries will not be extended. Micah 7:11 tells us, *"It will be a day for building your walls. On that day will your boundary be extended."* Are you sitting around praying the prayer of Jabez but still afraid to rise up and build? How long have you been waiting on the Lord to bless you? It is time for you to take the step of faith. You have to *do*. You have to build and then the Lord will reward your efforts.

"Jabez cried out to the God of Israel, 'Oh, that you would bless me and enlarge my territory! Let your hand be with me, and keep me from harm so that I will be free from pain.' And God granted his request (1 Chronicles 4:10, NIV). Do you think God

enlarged Jabez's territory without any action on his part? Faith without works is dead. God expects you and I to take action. Instead of being afraid, begin to build on a solid foundation. *"I also say to you that you are Peter, and upon this rock I will build My church; and the gates of Hades will not overpower it"* (Matthew 16:18, NASB).

There is no doubt that Jesus is the rock. *"For other foundation can no man lay than that is laid, which is Jesus Christ"* (1 Corinthians 3:11, NIV). Ask God for His guidance and when you ask, expect great things from Him but remember to *attempt* great things for God. It is what is expected of you. Jesus said in John 15:7-8, *"Ask whatever you wish, and it will be done for you. This is to my Father's glory, that you bear much fruit, showing yourselves to be my disciples."*

The key to building on the rock, the solid foundation, is to *"read the word, review the word, remember the word, and respond to the word."* (Rick Warren)[1]. Jesus said in Matthew 7:24 (NIV), *"Everyone who hears these words of mine and puts them into practice is like a wise man who built his house on the rock."* Your life and everything you do and build, must be built on the word of God in order for it to be sustainable. Otherwise, when the storms come, it will fall apart. The rock, Jesus Christ, the word, helps you to withstand all storms. Read the word and build.

Prayer

Father, I thank You for promising to help me. I thank You for giving me the autonomy to build and enlarge my territory. Lord, I would never want to build on sinking sand. Please help me to read Your Word daily, meditate on it, and make it a part of my life. Thank You for being my solid rock, my constant, and my shelter in the time of storm. You promised to help me through the storms of life. I trust You, Lord and honor You. In Jesus' name. Amen!

Testimony – Atarah Wright

Pushing through fear is one of the most rewarding experiences because it strengthens you. It increases your confidence. It builds your faith. When my faith is tested, I love to say, *"Keep it pushing."* Through all the struggles, challenges, and naysayers, I kept it pushing this past year to prove to myself that as long as God says yes, nobody can say no.

A short version of my testimony encompasses challenges I overcame last year. It is now 1/11/16 and I recall F.E.A.R., False Evidence Appearing Real, creeping up when we moved our family of six to Atlanta, GA. We were compelled to grow on another level of our dream lifestyle, in spite of the unknown challenges we would face. Imagine living a stable life, and an opportunity presents itself designed to yield the results we desired. I wanted to rebuild my coaching and real estate investing business. My husband wanted to find his dream job and continue working on building our fortune part time. We both felt it was time and it's exactly what we did.

Trusting God with every step, we made a faith move. Living with my mother plus four other grown folks along with my family, made 11 people in one house. It was a big beautiful mansion but it was still challenging at times. We had to put our seat belts on. We planned to save extra money for our next home and move out in six months. It seemed simple enough, right? Yet, God had another plan, plus some lessons for us to learn, and challenges for our family to overcome.

The second month in Georgia, our sweet baby girl who was rarely sick, was hospitalized for four days with an unknown upper respiratory viral infection. They didn't have a clear diagnosis. We were scared for her life. Do you think fear came up? Yes, it did. What did we do? We pushed through it! We prayed for healing and God was glorified.

Although I was grateful, the negative energy overtook me, which caused a delay in some of our plans. My business was stalled while I took care of what was most important, our daughter. My husband's new position was delayed, which meant we were spending savings to pay bills. Drama was unfolding in the house, which I had no control over, so it stressed me out. My fear was that this was going to be a longer ride than anticipated.

By the time I realized my environment was affecting me negatively, six months had gone by. I had to make a choice. I chose faith over fear. I practiced pushing harder. My strength grew. My relationship got stronger. I developed a closer relationship to God. I kept my eye on the prize. Before I knew it my husband would have his dream job and my Real Estate Investing and Coaching business would be thriving again.

By the end of summer 2015, almost one year later, the praying, fasting, and donating time and money began to payoff. I started to read motivational books, listen to empowering audio books, and watch my favorite inspiring speakers online. Every time something would occur, I just kept it pushing. To me, fear is not real, it is only in your mind. I knew without a shadow of a doubt that there was something bigger in store than I could ever plan.

My husband procured his dream job working for HUD in multifamily division as an Underwriting Analyst. I dusted off my losses of another failed attempt in business and found a Real Estate Investment Organization that took me under their wing and became my new family. The group is very supportive and provides the education in business and investing that helps its members push through fear of unknown wealth strategies.

Then the magic of a miracle began to unfold. I was able to realize some money I didn't know existed. We applied for a VA home loan. The application was denied. We needed a middle credit score of 620 to be approved. My husband had mid-score of 617. I was shocked his score was lower than expected, which happened because of a fraudulent account. Even the application for an apartment was denied.

I knew credit repair was in order so I reached out to my real estate investor family. The resources provided, allowed us to change our situation in a few months. Both our credit scores are now in the high 600's and low 700s. I raised $24K in one day, doing peer lending which are private investors loaning money instead of a traditional bank. I paid off $8,100 in credit card debt. The payments were about the same, however the term loan will be paid off in 2016, whereas making only minimum payments would take 20 years plus.

I was ecstatic that this new found credit building and financial strategy worked. My advanced real estate investing education was paying off! Next, I did a silent investor deal and made another $5K right before Christmas. God's plan was unfolding. I felt like we were being rewarded for pushing so hard to the next level. I could see the light at the end of the journey and it was as bright as can be.

On 12/23/2015, our 19th marriage anniversary, I

received a congratulatory letter of the preapproval for $250K to buy our new home. We are currently putting in offers for a next dream home. A real no money down deal is in the works. Once we purchase our home we plan to have it paid off within the next 10 years by implementing a rare, but creative mortgage acceleration strategy I learned from investing in financial and real estate investment education. I'm humbled and grateful for God's plan.

Atarah Wright
www.themagiccashlady.com
magiccashlady@gmail.com

Action Plan

Focus on the lesson for today. Then think on this quote: *"Sometimes God lets you hit rock bottom so that you will discover that He is the rock at the bottom"* (Tony Evans). Profound truth, isn't it? Your rock bottom experience is no excuse for you not to build. It's reason for you to trust God and seek His guidance. Meditate on your favorite passage of scripture and/or on Isaiah 41:13. Journal your thoughts and your experience below:

_____

_____

_____

CRY THROUGH THE FEAR

Scripture

"And God heard the voice of the lad; and the angel of God called to Hagar out of heaven, and said unto her, "What aileth thee, Hagar?" fear not, for God hath heard the voice of the lad where he is."
Genesis 21:17

Lesson

Hagar, being cast out of Abraham and Sarah's home, found herself wandering in the wilderness of Beer-Sheba with no water or food for her and her son, Ishmael. Being destitute, she wept profusely about the possible pending death of her son. Ishmael joined her as well in her weeping.

The Bible says, *"God heard the lad"* and spoke to Hagar through His angel. *"Fear Not"* he said, *"for the voice of the lad has been heard."* God then immediately showed Hagar a well of water and also told her that He would make Ishmael a great nation.

What destitute circumstances have you found yourself in? Have you solicited your family, even your children, to join you in prayer? Paul solicited help, as noted in Romans 15:30 (NIV). *"I urge you, brothers and sisters, by our Lord Jesus Christ and by the love of the Spirit, to join me in my struggle by praying to God for me."* Do not be afraid to solicit help for prayer. Much prayer, much power. Do not worry about finding the right words to say as you cry out to God in prayer. Remember Romans 8:26 says, *"In the same way, the Spirit helps us in our weakness. We do not know what we ought to pray for, but the Spirit himself intercedes for us through wordless groans."*

Cry through your fear. Don't bury your head in the pillow, with a no hope type of cry; but rather let it be a call upon the name of Jesus, my help in times past, my hope for years to come type of cry. Cry out with hope knowing your Heavenly Father hears and is ready and waiting to come to your rescue.

God has bigger things and plans in store for you than you can ever imagine. *"[He] is able to do exceeding abundantly above all that we ask or think, according to the power that worketh in us."* (Ephesians 3:20). Start thinking victory. Start turning those tears of sorrow into tears of joy. *"Weeping may endure for a night but joy comes in the morning"* (Psalm 30:5). Imagine morning has come. What does it look like for you? Do you see victory? Do you see the dry desert behind you and the beautiful Promised Land before you? God wants us to look to the bright future He has in store for us today. Cry tears of joy through your fears. Your victory is in sight.

Prayer

Dear God, thank You for Your Word that brings

hope and life to a hopeless and dying situation. Thank You for Your love; that perfect love that casts out all fear. Today Lord, I cry out to You with joy, knowing that my prayer ascends to You like sweet incense through Your son Jesus, by the Holy Spirit. Father, oftentimes I am lost for words, but I thank You for the Holy Spirit, who helps me in my weakness and intercedes for me. Many times Lord, I am afraid because of the situation I find myself in and the bleak look of the future. Help me not to focus so much on tomorrow, knowing that's Your problem and that You hold tomorrow in Your hands.

Help me to focus on today and surrender to You now. Right now I choose to cry tears of joy, hope, and victory to You Lord, knowing that just like You provided for Hagar and Ishmael in the desert, just like You feed the birds of the air, so much more will You provide for me. Thank You Father, in the name of Jesus. Amen!

Testimony – Lisa Chappell

She was dying and protecting her quality of life fell upon my shoulders. I was her little girl. I could barely take care of myself, let alone make decisions for my mother. We lived together since 1995 and even before then, I was only a brisk 7 minute walk from her house. She held many roles in my life besides mother. She was counselor, sounding board, personal coach, homie, comedian, top chef, and nutritionist. As with the change of seasons, I became her care taker. Mom's health declined due to kidney disease. As we moved along the painful path of hospital stays and emergency room visits, I was frightened. I was immobilized by fear of making the wrong decisions on my mom's behalf. Fear met me at every turn: upon waking— Fear. Speaking with doctors—Fear. Answering a call from the hospital—Fear. Fear met me at my front door as I walked in the house, afraid to face bad news. There she was, smiling and an interesting story to share was always right behind her smile. Despite her condition, a four course dinner was always warming in the oven.

One night, while taking a shower, I sobbed deep from within my soul. I was on my knees before God and prayed for strength and perseverance. I asked Him to take away the fear and replace it with faith. I prayed for direction and guidance in making the right decisions for my mom. From this moment, I was no longer fearful but faithful. The fire in my belly was alit with the love I had for my mom. I was empowered and equipped to bear the heaviest of burdens placed upon my shoulders. It was now the child's obligation to care for the parent and I honored the assignment.

Life is full of ironies. During what should have been the saddest of times, it was the happiest. The last six months of my mom's life were the most fulfilling. Our bond was tighter than ever and despite the reversal in care taker roles, the lines were never blurred on who was the parent and who was the child. Dialysis sessions were three times per week from 4am to 10am. I adjusted my hours at work to accompany my mom to all of her appointments, meet with doctors, fill prescriptions, and interview home healthcare aides. Whenever possible and only if mom was feeling up to it after dialysis treatments, we would spend time at the mall, go out to eat, or participate in any activity unrelated to hospitals.

There were more 'up' days than down ones, but when those down days showed up, fear took a back seat. My strength was my mom's comfort. My confidence and leadership were her peace. My loyalty as the daughter to her mother was joy. Emergency room visits became routine within the last two months of her life. Doctors and nurses were on first name basis and greeted us with hugs and kisses. I was given access to supply rooms and employee break rooms. My mom and I entertained ourselves with everything and everybody around us. Laughter is the best medicine. More often, I would work from home in order to be available to my mom if an emergency should arise. Never did it enter my mind that God was ready for her. That I would find her in eternally sleep in her favorite recliner in her bedroom. That in a blink of an eye she would simply be gone.

The funeral had passed and family, friends and mourners who I had never met returned to their lives.

I sat in the kitchen at the table where mom and I had eaten dinner together just one week ago when two words escaped my lips, shattering the heavy silence, *"now what?"* What do I live for now that my mom is gone? Who do I live for? I was alone. Before the familiar, bitter taste of fear began to form on the back of my tongue, the lesson I learned became very clear, God was showing me that the strength I prayed for was always inside of me.

Lisa Chappell
www.lisachappell4real.com
lisachappell100@gmail.com

Action Plan

Write about the situation(s) you are going through right now that's causing you to be fearful. Knowing that this too shall pass, write out your praise to God right now for what He will do for you as He takes you to the other side. Be blessed through the process!

_____

_____

_____

_____

_____

_____

DRIVE AWAY THE FEAR

Scripture
"Say to those with fearful hearts, "Be strong, do not fear; your God will come, He will come with vengeance, with divine retribution, He will come to save you." Isaiah 35:4

Lesson

When I think of vengeance, I think of great power and destruction; I envision that anything in the path will be totally destroyed beyond recognition. Wouldn't you love to have your fears be destroyed beyond recognition? If yes, then imagine with me.

God is moving on your behalf with Divine retribution, to devour anything or anyone that stands in your path, trying to prevent you from fulfilling His purpose in your life. Doesn't this boost your confidence a little knowing this is exactly what God says He will do for you?

God cares about every single aspect of your life. In Matthew 10:30 we are told that the very hairs on our head are all numbered. In verse 31, we are encouraged to not be afraid because we have more value than the many sparrows for which He cares.

Think a little further about Creation. God spoke the world and everything in it into being except for man. Instead He took the time to stoop down, take the dust of the ground and form man with His very own hands, and when He was done, He breathed His breath into man's nostrils and man became a living being. I don't know about you, but this is reassuring for me. God thought of every little detail and intricacy that goes into our conception and birth. He cares a lot for you and me. We are blessed and highly favored by Him.

So for you who feel lost, alone, confused, and discouraged, remember those are just lies the devil is planting in your mind to prevent you from doing something extraordinary in your life. The devil wants you to feel worthless as if you are never enough. You are more than enough with God. God can and will destroy those images and feelings from your life if you let Him. He will fight this battle for you against the enemy, with a vengeance. He wants to save you. Give Him permission. Surrender your feelings and your fears to Him and watch Him work on your behalf. Learn to live your life leaning on the everlasting arms of God.

Remember, you are blessed and highly favored by God. He loves you with an everlasting love. It is because of this love, you can be assured that He will save you from anything or anyone that stands in your way, even your very fears. Therefore, stand like the brave and embrace His mission for your life as you drive those fears away.

Prayer

Father, You are awesome. You have made provisions for every turn in my life. You recognized that down through the ages, I would be bombarded with the cares and concerns of life that would inevitably cause me to experience fear. I am bombarded with the fear of moving forward and of failing; fear of what people would think or say; and all sorts of other fears that the enemy has planted in my life to keep me from being obedient to Your call.

Daddy, because of Your promises to me, I release these fears from my life today and I drive them and the father of all fears and lies away, by the power of the Holy Spirit. Help me not to pick them back up but to continue to focus on the God that You are, who will always be with me. I pray this prayer in the precious name of Jesus. Amen!

Testimony – Glenise Harris-Wilson

I believe God's Word and the essence of His presence has been my guiding light. So often we tread in darkness blinded by the secrets of disappointments, low self-esteem, betrayal and hopelessness. We lose sight trying to make choices and decisions. We find ourselves handicapped with the inability to see the other side of the road as we travel to a place searching for meaning and purpose in our lives. Ultimately, we do not have to make these choices and decisions, if we allow God to take charge and root ourselves in faith, believing His promises. Our task of saying yes or no in our decision-making process rests in His hands.

Consequently, I resorted to my faith and meditated through prayer and fasting as I began to let go of my fear to step into my purpose. I recall the Scripture in the book of Isaiah, *"So do not fear, for I am with you; do not be dismayed, for I am your God. I will strengthen you and help you; I will uphold you with my righteous right hand"* Isaiah 41:10. Right at that moment I knew I had nothing to be afraid of. All I needed was the courage to say I will let Go and let God.

After being employed in Corporate America for 29 1/2 years, I found myself trying to overcome many midlife challenges a number of adults face. I was trying to balance work life and single parenting, as well as trying to find purpose in a job that was not fulfilling. I reached a point where I started to search for more until I realized I was searching for my purpose. My midlife years were challenging and overwhelming. However, I refused to get stuck. I knew there was something I was supposed to be connected with, where I would find solitude in my work and service I was born to provide. Yet, in order to get to see the light of this experience, I had to let go of something. I retired with no job or employment strategy. I only had God whom I relied on for direction, wisdom and knowledge to connect me with the "right" people and the "right" resources.

I knew I did not have the ability on my own to be selective because of my hunger and thirst to fulfill the passion of working with adults in midlife. I had to overcome challenges on my midlife journey such as a divorce, single parenting, being spiritually unmotivated, becoming a caretaker for ill/aging parents, dealing with parents death, empty-nester syndrome, career change, educational pursuits, chronic illness, remarriage, blended family, and retirement after 29 plus years from a Fortune 500 Company. God orchestrated my steps allowing me to birth and create Brighter Promises Life & Transformational Coaching, LLC.

I was afraid because for years I struggled with low self-esteem. Going through many challenges, I was left not feeling good about myself. I knew I wanted something greater. I knew I needed to release something within to feel the beauty of my worth. Deep down in my soul, I knew I was worthy. I even feared my age because I could not cross over from the barrier of feeling I was too old to do many things I aspired to do. I wasted months and years holding on to that feeling. I wanted to go back to school. I entered a doctoral program and now I am working on obtaining the Ed.D. at 59 1/2 years of age. I wanted to become an entrepreneur, speaker and a writer. Here I am today, walking in my purpose, aligned in my faith. I prayed for deliverance from the negative bondage of which I gave the enemy power.

Removing the fear and holding on to my faith, God did it. In Ecclesiastes 9:10, *"Whatever your hands find to do, do it with all your might."* The hand God has given me helps me help adults in midlife to transition into a spiritually balanced life. I help them do what I did and that is remove barriers that injected uncertainties and unhappiness. It is my desire that men and women become filled with the beauty of knowing God is a keeper of His promises and He will not let you down.

"In God's reality, the more you give of yourself--in feeling, generosity, self-expression, goodness, creativity, and love--the more you will be given." ~
Deepak Chopra

Glenise Harris-Wilson
2brighterpromises@gmail.com

Action Plan

Write down your fears. Get an accountability partner, a coach, or a mentor you can trust with your fears and concerns. Have that person help you develop a plan to move you beyond those fears and hold you accountable for executing the action plan.

SHINE THROUGH THE FEAR

Scripture

"Do not be afraid but let your hands be strong so you could be a blessing." Zechariah 8:13

Lesson

"Let your light so shine before men that they may see your good works and glorify your father which is in Heaven" (Matthew 5:6). There is no place for fear in shine. Shining reflects light. Fear is darkness. Fear is Satan trying to hide the light God has given you. When you allow your fears to take control, and overpower you, you are hiding your light. And Jesus said, *"You are the light of the world. A city that is set on a hill cannot be hidden. Nor do they light a lamp and put it under a basket, but on a lampstand, and it gives light to all who are in the house"* (Matthew 5:14-15, NKJV). Are you allowing fear to keep your light from shining and providing brightness to your household, community, and the world?

Stand up. Rise up. Shine your light. Shining your light means you act and react to situations in a different manner than the world. When you are too afraid to stand out in the crowd and be an example, you are preventing others from seeing their path clearer and denying them from seeing the glory of God. People need to hear your voice. People need to be blessed by your services. You are a witness for the Lord through your ministry.

Recognize however, in order to shine your light, there must be light within you. This must be the light of Jesus Christ. When you feed upon His word and meditate on it daily, the glory of God cannot help but permeate through you in your attitudes, words, and actions. When Jesus gave the command "let your light shine" He was speaking to His disciples. We are His disciples today.

These instructions are intended for whatever area of your life God is calling you, be it in church ministry, in business, or on the job. You have to see it as an integral part of God's plan. Until you do, success will evade you. I understand sometimes you may feel overwhelmed, like the calling is too big for you. These are the times God intends for you to seek strategic partnerships and form covenant relationships in order to finish His work here on earth. Do not let the size of the project scare you. Read Zechariah 8:23 and seek God for the right partner, the one who will shine right alongside you. God intended for us to work together to build His kingdom. Don't hide your talent. Don't let Satan blow it out. Shine it for Jesus until He comes.

Prayer

Father, I thank You for blessing me with gifts and talents. Help me to recognize that these gifts and talents are to be used for Your glory. When I allow fear to keep me from moving forward, I deny myself a blessing and someone else from being blessed as well. Teach me how to rely on You, as You promised to be with me and help me always. Father, help me to be bold for You. Help me to let my light shine before all men, in the area that You have called me to shine. In Jesus' name. Amen!

Testimony – Vanita Sanders

Imagine being 24 years old, married, pregnant and parenting a 4- year- old little girl. Now imagine being cheated on while you during this time, your husband leaving you and your children, and you are left to figure out life on your own. I do not have to imagine the scenario because I lived it. For three years I had to endure lonely nights, bill collectors because my two-income household had now been reduced to one, and attending solo prenatal appointments with the weight of the world on my shoulders. I left my parents' home at the tender age of 19. I vowed never to return because pride and shame would not let me. However, at this pivotal point in my life I wanted to run back to my childhood home, turn on some BET and wait for my mom to make dinner.

Wishful thinking! I knew this day would never come. It was my time to grow up, show up and take charge of my life. I was scared and unsure of what my next steps would be, but I knew my next few decisions would be life altering. My ex-husband leaving me and marrying his mistress changed me in many ways. It hardened my heart and gave me thicker skin, but it also gave me a better perspective about how God can push you to your destiny even in a crisis.

On October 21, 2006, I cried out to God and wrote in my journal that my life had to get better. There was no turning back on my dreams or the process. It was on this day I made the decision to sell my house, quit my job, and pack up my children to go back to college at the age of 27. The school was three hours away and I knew no one. What I did know was that my children and I deserved better. I had to push now more than ever before. My children were watching how I handled life's adversity. My responsibility as their mother was to show them when you are at your lowest, you can still walk with your head held high, stand tall, look adversity in the face, and win! I graduated within three years with honors and went on to receive my graduate degree from one of the top universities in the country. My journey is a testament to the power of resilience, prayer, and simply living life on your own terms. Adversity does not define you; it builds you into the person God wants you to be.

Vanita Sanders
www.notsorandomthoughtsofmamav.wordpress.com
giftedvisionsunlimited@gmail.com

RELEASING THE FEAR AND WALKING IN FAITH

Action Plan

1. There is a song that I learned from childhood and maybe you learned it too: This Little Light of Mine. These songs were taught to us for a reason, to guide us along life's paths. Adopt the words as you heed God's call.

2. Remember, *"God can turn your ordinary into extraordinary"* (Tony Evans). Journal how you are going to shine where you are called, whether it be at home, school, work, in your business, in your neighborhood, on social media, or to the world.

_____

_____

_____

_____

_____

_____

_____

_____

_____

_____

_____

_____

_____

_____

_____

SPEAK THROUGH YOUR FEAR

Scripture
"Do not be afraid, you worm Jacob, little Israel, do not fear, for I myself will help you," declares the LORD, your Redeemer, the Holy One of Israel."
Isaiah 41:14

Lesson

God is calling you to rescue His people from bondage in a number of ways. Whether it's financial, spiritual, relationship, health, or other bondage, their deliverance is tied to your purpose. You have specific tasks and duties to fulfill. God promised He would help you. God has placed that ministry in your heart, soul, and spirit, not for your own elevation but for His edification and for the benefit of His people. When are you going to stop being concerned you are not good enough, that you do not know enough, or that no one will listen to what you have to share? Do not be concerned with what to say or who would be receptive. God has a plan.

When God decided enough was enough and it was time for the Israelites to be freed from Egypt, He commissioned Moses to first go tell the Elders of Israel that God gave him the responsibility to carry out this mission. He was to go to Pharaoh to tell him to let God's people go. Moses was concerned the

Israelites would not believe him and he was not bold enough to go to Pharaoh so he questioned God, *"Who will I tell them sent me and how should I do such a thing when I am not eloquent in speech?"* God always has the answer.

God's first response to Moses in Exodus 3:12 was, *"I will be with you."* That is God's answer to you as well. He will be with you. Then God told Moses to tell the Israelites that "I AM" sent Him. When your audience hears this, the audience your message is intended for, their spirit will be moved and they will believe, just as the Israelites believed and listened to Moses. The Holy Spirit will ensure this.

Sometimes when we are called to a mission we do not have the total picture. You may be called to speak but you may not know what to speak about. That is okay. Don't be afraid to move forward. When you take a step of faith, God will fill in all the blanks. Don't worry about your stutter; don't worry about the slowness in your speech. God is the way maker. Use your voice for Him if that is what you are being called to do.

Contemplate the dialogue between God and Moses in Exodus Chapter 4. In verse 10, Moses said to the Lord, *"Pardon your servant, Lord. I have never been eloquent, neither in the past nor since you have spoken to your servant. I am slow of speech and tongue."* Then in verse 11 & 12, the Lord said to him, *"Who gave human beings their mouths? Who makes them deaf or mute? Who gives them sight or makes them blind? Is it not I, the Lord? Now go; I will help you speak and will teach you what to say."*

When God says, go, go. He will help you. Here's another promise in the Word, *"Surely you will summon nations you know not, and nations you do not know will come running to you, because of the Lord your God, the Holy One of Israel, for he has endowed you with splendor"* (Isaiah 55:5, NIV). What a promise! He has endowed you with splendor so go, be bold and speak through your fears!

Prayer

Lord, You said in Your word, there is nothing new under the sun. Anything You are asking me to do today, You have proven in the past that You will make a way. Help me to stand up and follow Your lead. Help me to let my voice be heard. Help me not to allow Your people to remain in bondage because I am too afraid to go and do and speak. Father, You said You would help me and teach me what to say. Help me Lord to believe and move forward in faith. You are the Great I Am. You are, were and always will be. Teach me how to accept Your calling even when I cannot see the whole picture. Help me to take my responsibility seriously and stop focusing on me, but rather focus on the freedom Your people will experience through my work and voice. Help me to listen to the Holy Spirit as

He speaks to me, so He can speak through me. Father, I thank You for trusting me with this mission. I accept and I move forward in faith. In Jesus' name. Amen!

Testimony – Precious Brown

October 8, 2008 was the first time I appreciated the air I breathed. The day started as many others had but something in me said, "Today is different." Little did I know it was the end to a new beginning. This is the day my ex-husband tried to kill me by putting a loaded gun to my chest and pulling the trigger; but God! After the incident my children and I went to live with my sister, so I could try to make sense of it all.

After talking with the children about the inevitable split, I stepped out on the patio and for the first time in my life, I could smell the air. I could feel the gentle breeze on my face. That's when the overwhelming fear set in. My worst nightmare had come true. After 16 years of marriage it was over in a split second. I had nowhere to go, no money, and the worst part, I was alone. I had no clue what to do so I cried and talked to God, a lot. After a few days I pulled myself together and started walking in the faith I had claimed for so long. With $.27 cents in my pocket, terrible credit and the belief that God would do what He said, I applied for an apartment.

That Friday I got the approval call and was told I would only need $117.27 to move in. They agreed to hold the apartment until my payday on Friday. After paying for the apartment, a friend blessed me with the money for a U-Haul truck and the next day I went to our old house grabbed the kids' clothes, my clothes, their beds, a table for them to eat on and my shotgun for protection. We moved in and the realization set in, aloneness. Terrified to leave my comfortable life and even more terrified to go back. With God, I pressed through this dark place and eight years later the children are grown, I am a certified life coach, The Divorcologist™, helping divorced women through the pain.

I am a published author of three interactive workbooks, *The Process of Change* and an inspirational speaker. Although my life did not turn out the way I planned it, I am positive that God's plan is still being fulfilled through my life. Be encouraged and know that no matter what it looks like in the natural realm, the spiritual realm is working for your good. Bury this scripture in your heart: Jeremiah 29:11, *"For I know the plans I have for you,"* declares the Lord, *"plans to PROSPER you and not to harm you, plans to give HOPE and a future"* (Emphasis Mine). Believe that God will do what He said He would do if you trust Him. I am living proof.

Precious Brown
www.powercoachprecious.info
powerinyoullc@gmail.com

Action Plan

Meditate on the verse below and then write out what you have been called to speak about and whom your message is for. Don't always think it has to be a large audience but don't limit yourself to small either. Let the Spirit work through you.

Luke 4:18 (NIV) reads, *"The Spirit of the Lord is on me, because he has anointed me to proclaim good news to the poor. He has sent me to* proclaim *freedom for the prisoners and recovery of sight for the blind, to set the oppressed free."*

_____

_____

_____

_____

_____

_____

_____

_____

_____

_____

_____

_____

_____

_____

TRUST OVER THE FEAR

Scripture

"When I am afraid, I will trust in thee. In God I will praise His word, in God I have put my trust; I will not fear what flesh can do unto me."
Psalm 56: 3-4 and 10-11

Lesson

Many times we allow what people think and say about us, the lack of support or even the ridicule, to cripple us from moving forward with the vision and purpose God has for our lives. The response we get, or the lack thereof, can be very disheartening. David felt the pressure too. He felt oppressed by the Philistine people. He felt like they would swallow him up because they were so many.

It is easy to give up when you feel like it's you against the masses. It is very scary to venture out without the support of those you think matter most. The person who should matter most, the person who does matter most, is God and if God calls you to it, He will certainly take you through it. Greater is He that is in you than he that is in the world (1 John 4:4).

To trust God is to know He is a good God, who loves you and has the power to help you and pull you through every circumstance. Even more than having the power to help, know that He *wants to* and that He *will* help you. Proverbs 3:5-6 (NKJV) says, *"Trust in the Lord with all your heart, and lean not on your own understanding; in all your ways acknowledge Him, and He shall direct your paths."*

When you are in need, trust God. When you don't know which way to turn, trust God. When your life is in turmoil, trust God. When people speak ill of you and try to discourage and discredit you, trust God. When others forsake you, trust God. He is the Alpha and the Omega, the beginning and the end. He is the one who made you and fashioned you in His likeness. He is your shield and buckler. He is the one who *will supply all your needs,* [especially what you need to fulfill His calling on your life], *according to His riches in glory in Christ Jesus* (Philippians 4:19). In all things, trust Him.

Prayer

Dear God, I trust You. Even when I cannot trace you Lord, I trust You. Even when I feel alone, I trust You. Even when I am scared, Lord I will trust You. You have directed us, through your word, to trust in the Lord with all our hearts and lean not unto our own understanding, in all our ways we should acknowledge You and You will direct our paths. Lord, I believe and I accept that You will be my guide. Help me to keep my eyes fixed on You and only You. In Jesus' name. Amen!

Testimony – Jamella Stroud

We in the Christian community are more than able to tell others and ourselves the "What's" of the Bible but have a hard time explaining the "How's." Let us take faith for instance. We can quote the Bible based on what is stated in Hebrews 11:1. *"Faith is the substance of things hoped for and the evidence of things not seen."* Yes, this is the definition of faith, but how does it look for you or me?

I was the person who could tell others all the "What's" of the Bible, but I did not have any experiences for myself to speak about the "how" until my life was faced with a crisis. After being in business five years, everything appeared to be going well for me. This is until the business that became my financial safe haven was the very thing I was praying to God about, asking Him to save. It was going downhill fast. I was sure I was a woman of faith. I prayed, fasted, studied the Bible, led Bible studies, I could quote the Bible with the best of them. I didn't understand what was happening or where I went wrong. One day my answer arrived. My faith was based on me holding on to what I wanted as an outcome, instead of letting go and allowing God's outcome to manifest in my life.

To have faith is to trust God with the outcome of any given situation even when things appear to be going wrong. Abraham was willing to let go of what he wanted, which was a son and sacrifice him as God asked. He let go and pressed forward. Rahab, who hid the spies, was willing to let go of what she wanted, her life and hide the spies, even in the face of death. Jesus let go of His divinity and came to earth as humanity because He trusted His Father.

I too had to let go of what I wanted as an outcome and after doing so, it has been such a blessing in my life. Although I envisioned something different, I welcome the new turn my business has taken. In fact, I now experience less stress and a freedom that I never knew. I earned a designation in my field that allows me the ability to do what I truly dreamed of in my field. I am learning that "Faith/Trust" in God is not an overnight thing. There are some areas we trust God with more than others and He knows those areas. He continues to draw us in relationship with Him until we trust Him with our whole self and everything in us. If there's an idea, thing, or person you are holding on to that's keeping you stuck, I encourage you to let go and have faith in God's outcome.

Jamella Stroud
jamellastroud@gmail.com

Action Plan

List the things in your life that you must trust God

for and then end with, "I will trust you Lord."
For Example:
- For debt elimination, I will trust you Lord.
- For that husband (or wife) I've been praying and waiting for, I will trust you Lord.

WORSHIP THROUGH THE FEAR

Scripture

"Fear thou not, for I am with thee: be not dismayed, for I am thy God: I will strengthen thee; yea, I will help thee; yea I will uphold thee with the right hand of my righteousness." Isaiah 41:10

Lesson

The God of the Universe commands us not to fear. This same God is The One who spoke the world into being; The One who parted the Red Sea; The One who calmed the seas; and The One who fed 5,000 men with five loaves and two fish. This very same God, with all of this power and might, promised to be with us, so there is no need to be afraid. We can be confident that God's promises are true and sure because in 2 Peter 3:9, we are assured God is not slack concerning His promises. Whatever God says He will do, He will do. So do not fear, He will be with you at every turn and in all circumstances.

Sometimes in life when things do not go as planned, we get distressed and start to worry. With God on your side, there is no need to worry. Whatever it is you might be dealing with, remember ALL things work together for good to them that love God, to them who are called according to His purpose (Romans 8:28). So when you are going through, call upon God, the very God who promised to strengthen you, to help you and uphold you. He will.

Here are two additional passages of Scripture to ponder as you seek to worship God in spite of the perplexing situation you might find yourself in.

1. 1 Pet 4:12-13 (NIV): *"Dear friends, do not be surprised at the painful trial you are suffering, as though something strange were happening to you. But rejoice that you participate in the sufferings of Christ, so that you may be overjoyed when his glory is revealed."*

Note: God is getting ready to reveal something to you. Hang tight.

2. Ps 66:8-12 (NIV) *"Praise our God, O peoples, let the sound of his praise be heard; he has preserved our lives and kept our feet from slipping. For you, O God, tested us; you refined us like silver. You brought us into prison and laid burdens on our backs. You let men ride over our heads; we went through fire and water, but you brought us to a place of abundance."*

Receive He will bring you to a place of abundance in your ministry, your finances, your health, your child-bearing, your marriage, or in your business.

There is victory at the end of the storm you are going through. Don't give up. Don't give in. Start worshiping God today and preparing your testimony now.

Yes, praise Him through your present situation. Give Him the glory He deserves. Remember when the praises go up, then the blessings come down. God inhabits our praise. Worship the fear away.

Prayer

God, I thank You for Your revelation to me today. Father, I praise and honor You, I magnify Your Name because of who You are. Lord, because of who You are and because of whose I am, I bind all fear that is within me and I release my faith in You, not by my own strength dear God but by the strength You promised through Christ Jesus (Philippians 4:13). God, Your word says in 2 Corinthians 5:7 that we live by faith, not by sight, and so Lord, I choose today to focus on the unseen realities, to trust You in every circumstance and to glorify You in all I do. In the mighty name of Jesus. Amen!

Testimony – LaToya Rose

My success story is powered by Luke 12:48 (KJV): *"But he that knew not, and did commit things worthy of stripes, shall be beaten with few stripes. For unto whomsoever much is given, of him shall be much required: and to whom men have committed much, of him they will ask the more."*

When I was ten years old, I made a list of what I expected from life's journey (as far as I could imagine at the time). Listed were things like: retire at age forty, become a billionaire, be an award winning author, have a large home with a pool, have awesome friends, be married with a mate that is God-fearing, financial abundant, a sharp dresser, and embody the seven Fruit of the Spirit genuinely.

In my younger years, I knew that there was something unique about my purpose; however, it was not until 2009 that I realized just how much I was destined for greatness. During this summer, the truth around my conception was revealed and what a blow it had on my mental, spiritual, and physical health. All I held true for about five years was, "my mother gave birth to a predator's child; how dare that man take advantage of her." It was unfortunate that during these five years I isolated and even considered myself "emancipated" from my family. I had adopted the "independent woman syndrome," the part of the syndrome where strangers are more valuable than your God-given family.

The turning point for me was when it came time for me to start my consulting business in July 2014. I was depleted financially and all these "friends" that once enjoyed my company (money) were nowhere to be found. Although we know the saying, *"it's better to give than receive,"* I had not given to people of good character thus not sowing seeds on good grounds. While blinded in addiction, abuse, and anger, I fell flat on my face. It only took three months for the people around me to rob me senseless. The day, I woke up in vomit and urine with blurred vision, that was it for me. I was tired of killing myself softly and thankfully awakened to realize that God did care about my immediate confusion or lack of self-love. He had not left but had a plan to turn these messes into a message in due time.

After five years of running from purpose, I have embraced that my conception is not my sentence to misery. Instead, it was the gateway for me to be an agent of change, hope, and resilience. Yes, my life could have been aborted but it was not; therefore, I could not allow that incident to cause me to question my existence because God makes no mistakes.

The minute I re-positioned myself in the Kingdom and joined a Bible-based, Spirit-filled community I began to flourish in my business and great things have been manifesting every day. This constant manifestation could only occur once I stopped trying to change my past.

Remember, it is during the various temporary pits of character reconstruction when one learns the true value of "obedience is better than sacrifice." Just P.U.S.H. - Pray Until Something Happens. You will gain the victory. When fear attempts to suck you into a sinkhole of despair. Don't allow it to. Sing for hope, praise and worship for peace, give for prosperity, love for God loves you and shine brighter than your past because your territory has been enlarged.

LaToya Rose
www.latoyarose.com
connect@latoyarose.com

Action Plan

Journal what you're feeling in your spirit right now. Worship God for what He has done for you in the past, for what He is doing for you today, and for what He will do for you in the future.

_____

_____

_____

_____

_____

_____

_____

_____

_____

_____

_____

_____

_____

GIVE THROUGH THE FEAR

Scripture

"Do not be afraid, you wild animals, for the pastures in the wilderness are becoming green. The trees are bearing their fruit; the fig tree and the vine yield their riches." Joel 2:22

Lesson

I love stories and the lessons gleaned from them. At church one Sabbath, the person officiating during the collection of the offering shared the following story:

Someone once said there are three types of givers in life. One type is a flint, another is a sponge, and the third is a honeycomb. To get anything out of the flint, it must be hammered; even then, all the results are chips and sparks. To get anything out of the sponge, it must be continually squeezed and put under pressure. Finally, there is the honeycomb, just overflowing with its own sweetness. We can apply this analogy to our hearts. Sometimes, like the flint, God needs to work in our hearts in a difficult way in order for us to receive his goodness and then give it out. Sometimes, like a sponge, God needs to squeeze us and put pressure on us to bring forth any life from our hearts. Other times, like the honeycomb, we come to understand the goodness and grace of God, and love for other people overflows from our full hearts.

This beautiful excerpt was from the book *Overcoming* by Steve Mays[2].

God loves a cheerful giver. He expects us to plant seeds of giving and when we do, especially when we ourselves do not have it, our harvest will be plenty. Luke 6:38 (NIV) says, *"Give, and it will be given to you. A good measure, pressed down, shaken together and running over, will be poured into your lap. For with the measure you use, it will be measured to you."*

I can give a personal testimony of the blessings of giving. One Sunday night, several years ago, I was invited to a church to sing. The church had a project they were working on and solicited the congregation to give towards that project. I had my last $10 in my pocket, which needed to take me through the week because payday was not until that Friday. The Holy Spirit kept prompting me to give. In my mind I kept looking at the money and then looking at the week ahead. All I could see was how the $10 was not even enough and so if I gave it, what would I do? Over and over again, I played this scene in my head. However, the Holy Spirit kept prompting me to give. Right then I remembered my aunt giving a similar story of facing that same struggle and how she was rewarded for her obedience in giving. That was the Holy Spirit at work again by jogging my memory.

Without giving it another thought, I pulled out the $10 bill and threw it in the offering plate. I felt such a weight lifted off of me when I did that but of course I quickly retreated and went right back to questioning myself. Are you crazy? How can you be at ease when you have nothing to take you through the week? That's exactly how Satan works. He tries to keep us from what God is calling us to do and then when we muster up enough courage and faith to do it, he makes us question ourselves. Yet there is always that still soft voice we need to listen to and be in tune with. I heard that voice that night saying, "it is going to be alright." At the end of the service, the person who invited me to the church to sing that night walked over to me, thanked me for coming, and handed me a check for $50. Praise God! I got $10 for each day of the workweek. Isn't God amazing? Shouldn't we always trust Him?

You might be going through some financial challenges and I know it can be frightening. I am writing from experience. It's scary. Do not let Satan get the upper hand on your situation. Do not allow him to tell you to hold on to God's tithes and offerings. Do not let him keep you from giving where the Holy Spirit is calling you to give. Do not be afraid to plant seeds. The blessing is in the giving. It is in trusting God. God is testing you in this. Malachi 3:8 cautions about mere mortals who rob God in tithe and offerings and then in verse 10 (NIV), God instructs us to, *"Bring the whole tithe into the storehouse, that there may be food in my house. Test me in this,"* says the LORD Almighty, *"and see if I will not throw open the floodgates of heaven and pour out so much blessing that there will not be room enough to store it."* God knew it would be a test but He promised blessings overflowing as a reward. Trust God today, give, and see His glory revealed.

Prayer

Father, I thank You for examples in the Bible and in our current lives that teach us the rewards for trusting You. Lord, I choose today to trust You. I choose to believe that You can and that You will provide for all my needs according to Your riches in glory. Thank You for being the ultimate Father who is rich in houses and lands and who does not withhold good things from Your children.

Help me not to hold back but to give as the Holy Spirit prompts. Lord, I recognize that Your timing is not my timing, so please help me not to be anxious about my current financial situation but to be grateful today for Your provisions and look forward in anticipation for what You will do for me once I remain faithful. Thank you Lord. In Jesus' name. Amen!

Testimony – Valerie Priester

I can recall as if it was yesterday. One Sunday morning in 1986 I was in church and it was our church's anniversary. The Pastor had asked every member to give $100 to support the church's anniversary. Now $100 doesn't sound like much but to me it felt like $1,000.

At the time I was a single mother, divorced for one year. I was working two jobs, and dealing with my child's father who was irresponsible with his obligations for non-custodial support. I worked seven days a week, most of these days were between 12 – 14 hours. My daughter was seven years old at the time. I remember having to split a can of Pork-n-Beans with my daughter three or four times a week because it was all I could afford. I had some support from my mother, my grandmother, and an aunt that lived in the town we had relocated to, but even with their support it was at times very slim.

When I think back over this time in my life I remember the silver lining being present but unfortunately hard for me to see. My little angel, my daughter, always reminded me. The silver lining was my daughter never felt deprived, poor, or lacking for anything. In fact, because of my part-time job as a manager with the children's retail clothing store OshKosh B'Gosh, all of my daughter's clothes were of this brand so her friends thought we were rich. Although this was good for my daughter at the time, it later proved to be a big problem. Because my daughter never really saw the struggles I had to endure to provide for her, she developed a sense of entitlement. She was very spoiled to say the least.

Getting back to the request for $100, the Pastor gave us two months to meet this request. For two months I tried my best to save. This request seemed to be impossible as I struggled to keep food on my table. On the Sunday the money was due, I sat in church thinking, *"there is no way I can do this, all I have in my bank account right now is my rent money."*

I had been taught about the spiritual principle of sowing and reaping but I had never really put it to the test as the Bible tells us to in Malachi 3:10. The truth is, I was always too afraid to give from the little I had – there was never any extra, I was living pay check to pay check.

On this day I made a decision to trust God and His word. I said a prayer as I pulled out my checkbook to write a check for $100. I knew that if God did not keep His promise I would be short $100 for my rent. This was a life defining moment for me. I had worked very hard to support me and my daughter. I never really trusted God enough to put my money on the line for real. So this day was the day I was drawing the line in the sand and placing a demand on my faith. I wrote the check and placed it in the offering basket. My heart was pounding but I felt a sense of calm deep within. I felt a knowing that everything would be alright. To my surprise, I did not start thinking about where I could get this $100 to make up the shortage on my rent. I was truly at peace.

The result of trusting God and activating my faith was not only the return of the $100 but a reward of $200. This taught me God is real and more important our faith produces results. This was the start of my unwavering belief in my faith to accomplish anything I desire in life. Today, I live by faith.

Valerie Priester
www.victoriouslifecoaching.com
valeriep@victoriouslifecoaching.com

Action Plan

1. Locate the song, *"Give to the Lord"* by Ron Kenoly and focus on the words.

2. Meditate on Matthew 6:25-34. *"Therefore I say unto you, take no thought for your life, what ye shall eat, or what ye shall drink; nor yet for your body, what ye shall put on. Is not the life more than meat, and the body than raiment? Behold the fowls of the air: for they sow not, neither do they reap, nor gather into barns; yet your heavenly Father feedeth them. Are ye not much better than they? Which of you by taking thought can add one cubit unto his stature? And why take ye thought for raiment? Consider the lilies of the field, how they grow; they toil not, neither do they spin:*

And yet I say unto you, that even Solomon in all his glory was not arrayed like one of these. Wherefore, if God so clothe the grass of the field, which today is, and tomorrow is cast into the oven, shall he not much more clothe you, O ye of little faith? Therefore take no thought, saying, What shall we eat? or, What shall we drink? or, Wherewithal shall we be clothed? (For after all these things do the Gentiles seek:) for your heavenly Father knoweth that ye have need of all these things. But seek ye first the kingdom of God, and his righteousness; and all these things shall be added unto you. Take therefore no thought for the morrow: for the morrow shall take thought for the things of itself. Sufficient unto the day is the evil thereof."

3. Write your thoughts and plans to move beyond the fear of giving and the crippling thoughts of what tomorrow holds, to having faith and trusting that God will provide. As you ponder, remember that He promised to abundantly bless those who give.

_____

_____

_____

_____

FIGHT THROUGH THE FEAR

Scripture

"You will not have to fight this battle. Take up your positions; stand firm and see the deliverance the LORD will give you, Judah and Jerusalem. Do not be afraid; do not be discouraged. Go out to face them tomorrow, and the LORD will be with you."
2 Chronicles 20:17

Lesson

Fear keeps you trapped in worry. It is a feeling of defeat. That feeling is of the enemy and not of God. The Bible is laced with scripture that is geared towards helping us fight our fears. Here are a few.

- Psalm 27: 1 - *The LORD is my light and my salvation; whom shall I fear? The LORD is the stronghold of my life; of whom shall I be afraid?*
- Psalm 27:5 - *For in the time of trouble he shall hide me in his pavilion: in the secret of his tabernacle shall he hide me; he shall set me up upon a rock.*
- Psalm 34:4 - *I sought the Lord, and he heard me, and delivered me from all my fears.*

Recognize God for who He is. He is the Creator of the Universe and Lord of everything; therefore you have no need to be afraid. When you focus on God as your protector and your shelter in the times of storm, you can be at peace during those turbulent times. Follow David's example, submit your fears unto God and He will hear and answer your prayers and bring relief from those fears. God tells us in 1 Timothy 6:12 to fight the good fight of the faith. Yes I know this is a scary command in the midst of turbulence and in the heat of the battle. However, God did not leave you stranded to fight on your own. He provided all you need to step boldly on the battlefield. He is going to be there for us and with us, but He also expects us to do some preparation. Here's the defense God offers.

Ephesians 6:10-18 gives us strict instructions on how we should prepare for battle. Take some time to read it now. It outlines that as our defense, we should put on the whole armor of God, which is comprised of seven components.

First, the belt of truth buckled around your waist. The belt represents stability and secures the other pieces of the armor. The truth spoken here is the word of God so we are to arm or immerse ourselves in the word of God. Jesus Himself when tempted by the devil was able to quote scripture because He was familiar with them. Become familiar with the word of God.

Second, the breastplate of righteousness in place. The breastplate provides protection for the vital organs of the body, especially the heart and lungs, which if damaged could be fatal. Righteousness means doing what is right in the eyes of God and being obedient to His commandments, not one time but continually.

Third, your feet fitted with the readiness that comes from the gospel of peace. In essence, your feet fitted means that it is protected with shoes. Without shoes you would be concerned about where you put your feet but with shoes you can now release the fear of debris and focus your attention on the battle at hand. The feet are connected with the gospel as found in Romans 10:15, *"How beautiful are the feet of those who preach the gospel of peace, who bring glad tidings of good things!"* The gospel of peace represents the good news of Jesus Christ, His saving grace, and the plan of redemption. When you focus on this good news it will bring you peace.

Fourth, the shield of faith with which you can extinguish all the flaming arrows of the evil one. This calls for big trust because you are hoping for something you have not yet seen. In order to fully trust God, you have to truly spend time examining Him to validate that His word is true and constant. When you walk in that trust and hold on to it, the evil one will not be able to stand against you and win.

Fifth, the helmet of salvation. The helmet protects the head from damage. It is a symbol for the protection of your mind from the stresses of the world. Salvation means saving or delivering you from something, that is, sin and its consequences, death. It is a gift from God. Once you fully commit to following God's plan and His way, you will not lose the battle, you will receive salvation. Free your mind. Focus on God's saving grace.

Sixth, the sword of the Spirit. This is the word of God. The Bible says in Hebrews 4:12, *"For the word of God is living and powerful, and sharper than any two-edged sword, piercing even to the division of soul and spirit, and of joints and marrow, and is a discerner of the thoughts and intents of the heart."* The battle you are fighting is a fierce one so you need to arm yourself with the sword, the word of God.

Seventh, pray. You should be in constant prayer to your Heavenly Father. Philippians 4:6 (NKJV) says, *"Be anxious for nothing, but in everything by prayer and supplication, with thanksgiving, let your requests be made known to God."* And Matthew 7:7-8 (NKJV) says, *"Ask, and it will be given to you; seek, and you will find; knock, and it will be opened to you. For everyone who asks receives, and he who seeks finds, and to him who knocks it will be opened."* God is eagerly waiting your call so He can respond and supply all your needs according to His riches in glory.

You have all you need to fight the good fight of faith. God has made it plain. Put on the whole armor of God.

Prayer

Dear Father, I thank You for being the God of the universe who thought about every intricate part of my being, the walk I would have to take through life, and made provisions to guide me and mold me. Through Your son Jesus, You made me worthy to be called Your son or daughter. Thank You for giving me the tools necessary to fight in this battle called life. Help me to stay in Your word, be obedient to Your commands, and trust You even where I cannot trace You. Help me to proclaim the good news of salvation and to pray without ceasing. Thank You for Your promises. In Jesus' name. Amen!

Testimony – Rasheena Perry

"Yea, though I walk through the valley of the shadow of death, I will fear no evil: for thou art with me; thy rod and thy staff they comfort me. Thou preparest a table before me in the presence of mine enemies: thou anointest my head with oil; my cup runneth over. Surely goodness and mercy shall follow me all the days of my life: and I will dwell in the house of the LORD forever" (Psalms 23:4-6).

"All my life I had to Fight" (Spielberg), one of the familiar phrases I often quote from the movie *"The Color Purple."* These words still ring in my ear, after almost 31 years. I was twelve years old as he stood towering over my small frame. Each time it happened,

I was afraid, but I kept fighting through my fear. Accustomed to his fondling and constant whispers in my ear, tonight his eyes were different, but just like he said nobody cared. So I closed my eyes, and I began to pray asking God to draw me near. Fighting through my fears is my life's story; the previous words only speak to how the fight for my mind, body and soul all began. At a time when other young girls were playing, I was being molested and taken advantage of.

As a child, the words fight and fear were suggestive of sorrow; my innocent ignorance associated them with pain. The experience gave my notions credence. At school, I would be a child and at home, I was forced to perform the duties of an adult. The bad memories I would try to hide, but little did I know how close the spirit of fear was to taking my mind. I taught myself how to read because my grandparents didn't know how. With nothing more than the Bible, I would read before I lay down. After a while, I no longer needed the book, the verses were now sketched in my head.

In 1993, I gave God my life, and despite my pain, I continued to serve. Sunday after Sunday, singing from the depths of my heart, emptying myself, His Spirit I sought to impart. "Use me for your service Lord in the midst of all my pain. I will forever sing your praise and bring Glory to your Matchless name. The enemy can take my body, but He will never steal my worship or my praise." These were the weapons I used to fight every day. All the while hearing the nagging voices, experiencing the flashbacks of the painful memories, reminding me that I was nothing and my life had no meaning. I fought with everything in me. It was the one thing I knew how to do. Down on my knees, I'd find my way, trusting God to see me through.

"Fight through the Fear," and you shall win. God knew the plans He had for me and He knew that I would win. Once I accepted the mantle He assigned to me, the word fight took on a brand new meaning. The fight was my weapon and fear was my fuel, and both pushed me into my passion. I developed courage and tenacity to go after the lost. I was created to be an example of strength to others and I was destined to win. My purpose was tied up in those two words, and the weight of His Glory was now guiding me. If it wasn't for the fight that ignited me, where would I be? From birth the enemy wanted to destroy me, but he never had a chance. Those tests and trials were sent to make me the Giant Slayer I am. The enemy stole from me things no child or woman should be forced to lose. When I count the cost, it was worth the loss. God gave me love, restored and renewed. In His image were you created, and in His likeness you can remain the same. Just fight through your fear and He will make you brand new; from existing to living again.

Rasheena Perry
rasheenaunscripted@gmail.com

Action Plan

How do you plan to implement what you have learned above? Write it down. Get an accountability partner, a fellow soldier in battle. Together, arm yourselves with the armor found in Ephesians 6:10-18.

_____

_____

_____

_____

_____

_____

_____

_____

_____

_____

_____

_____

_____

_____

_____

_____

_____

_____

PERSEVERE THROUGH THE FEAR

Scripture

"Do not be afraid of the king of Babylon, whom you now fear. Do not be afraid of him, declares the LORD, for I am with you and will save you and deliver you from his hands." Jeremiah 42:11

Lesson

According to Webster's Dictionary, perseverance is the quality that allows someone to continue trying to do something even though it is difficult. It is continued effort to do or achieve something despite difficulties, failure, or opposition. Another word for perseverance is steadfastness. 1 Corinthians 15:58 (KJV) says, *"Therefore, my beloved brethren, be ye stedfast, unmoveable, always abounding in the work of the Lord, forasmuch as ye know that your labour is not in vain in the Lord."* Perseverance in action is a call from God.

The story of the Chinese bamboo tree as told by Zig Ziglar is a perfect example of perseverance. *"When this particular seed is planted, watered and nurtured, for years it doesn't outwardly grow as much as an inch. Nothing happens for the first year. There's no sign of growth. Not even a hint. The same thing happens – or doesn't happen – the second year.*

And then the third year, the tree is carefully watered and fertilized each year, but nothing shows. No growth. No anything. So it goes as the sun rises and sets for four solid years. The farmer and his wife have nothing tangible to show for this labor or effort. Then, along comes year five. After five years of fertilizing and watering have passed, with nothing to show for it – the bamboo tree suddenly sprouts and grows eighty feet in just six weeks! Did the little tree lie dormant for four years only to grow exponentially in the fifth? Or, was the little tree growing underground, developing a root system strong enough to support its potential for outward growth in the fifth year and beyond? The answer is, of course, obvious. Had the tree not developed a strong unseen foundation it could not have sustained its life as it grew." What an amazing story.

Have you been working hard at something and just not seeing the results you are looking for? Do you feel doubtful and discouraged? Are others questioning why you continue with that something? In the meantime, in the midst of all this disappointment and unfruitfulness, you are noticing other trees, (individuals), growing, (prospering), like wild fire all around you. Think of the Chinese bamboo tree. Don't be envious of the runner next to you, just run your race. Keep nurturing. Keep watering. You may not see signs of progress now but continue to pour your heart and soul into it and keep building. God is causing a powerful "bamboo root system" to grow inside of you. This kind of root is strong and with a solid foundation, the kind that will outlast the storms of life. Continue to work hard and be committed. Do not give up. Stand in faith for that something that God has placed in your heart. Your little tree is growing underground and your gigantic tree will grow rapidly in due season. Persevere!

Prayer

Dear God, there is none like You. You even use nature to teach us life lessons. Only an infinitely wise God could have seen through the ages what life here on this sinful earth would be like for Your children. Lord, You set such examples in nature like the Chinese bamboo tree to teach us perseverance and other valuable lessons in life. You are an amazingly mighty and powerful God and I praise You for who You are. I worship You Lord. I thank You Father for Your provision for me. Help me to stand firm even when I cannot prove or qualify. That is a true measure of faith. Lord help me to be faithful in all things and know that life is not about quick fixes but about me being obedient to You as You work in the background to complete the work of salvation for Your children. Bless me indeed Lord for my steadfastness. In Jesus' name. Amen!

Testimony – Mary Lindsey

A story of faith being tested – and some say God is not concerned with every single detail of our lives. I went through a period of disappointment that saw me without my home, no job and a broken relationship – all in 2009. I was ready to give up.

What the atheists were saying must be true. How could He exist when He allowed all these "things" I had worked hard for to be taken away? I was done with God, but no matter how I tried to ignore God's presence, something kept me praying and hoping for a change. I finally decided to let go and let God. I packed it all in and after praying earnestly, the thought came to me to pack up and leave what many consider the greatest city on earth – NYC! Yet with my journey out of the area I had first called home in America, my only regret was leaving my daughter and some family members I had grown very attached to.

I bought a one-way ticket out of New York's LaGuardia airport for an early morning flight into Anchorage, Alaska. One-way because this move was going to be permanent. I would visit family and friends, but I was going to call Alaska my home, my permanent home. I had no job, no permanent place to live and only knew a few people in rural Alaska. Some may call it a bad move, but there was something pulling me away from the Lower 48s to the Last Frontier, and while I was not physically showing any resistance, I was torn and confused about the decision.

Three days before I was due to travel to Alaska, like Jonah I took a detour to an interview with the University of Central Florida – still doubting God. I had taken a flight just for the interview, rented a car for the day and would be traveling back from Florida that evening. I gave my all, but there was something lacking, something missing and on my drive down I-4 highway that runs through central Florida, I burst into tears and poured out my heart to God asking Him to please help me understand why I was, at this stage in my life, trying to find a job and home. I cried. Anyone looking on would have thought I was insane or had received some extremely bad news.

My flight from Florida departed on time, and 2 hours later I was getting to my vehicle that was left in short-term parking. Putting my purse on the passenger seat, I reached for my mobile phone and switched it on – it was turned off during the flight. I had two messages, one from a known phone number and the other call was unknown. I listened to each call in turn with the unknown call the last voicemail I listened to. And what I heard filled me with a better understanding of who my God really is and what He does in answer to our prayers.

The caller was an HR Administrator at a company in Anchorage, Alaska. About 3-5 months before I had applied with this company and had not accepted the interview at the time as the salary was below what would meet my needs. When I heard the name of the company I sighed as I believed the call was just another way to get me to accept the salary package, something I was not willing to do. In this turmoil in my head I could almost hear my Savior saying, 'I know the plans I have for you' and so right there in the parking lot at the airport I returned the telephone call.

We exchanged pleasantries and her words to me solidified for me that no matter the struggle, I should trust God. The HR Administrator indicated that the department was under new management and they would like to conduct a Skype interview with me the following week. I was amazed, as was the HR Administrator when I said that I would be traveling to Anchorage in a couple of days and would be glad to meet with the manager in person.

No place to stay, but God provided. A friend with whom I previously worked, was staying in Anchorage and was due to go to the hospital for some tests. He had a vehicle and would have put it in storage. However, with me in town, he allowed me to drive the vehicle to and from the interview location, to have my employment tests done and to try and find a place to stay. Who else but God would put things in place like this? Some may say this was all coincidental, but my God is organized. He always has a plan B when I act on my own devices and ruin plan A.

1. I stepped out on faith and behaved like I had a job and a place to live in Alaska when I purchased a one-way ticket to Anchorage.

2. Even when I went for the interview in Florida and had to cry out to God in despair, He didn't punish me. He loves me; He heard my cry and answered my prayer.

3. I had no place to stay in Anchorage, but God allowed my friend to be there, even though the circumstances were less than pleasant for him, to help me through the transition and to make my travel to and from the interview easier and with minimal stress.

4. I found a church and a pastor with family connections living in Anchorage and he became my landlord.

5. I was compensated for traveling to the interview and so had money to do everyday things.

6. I got the job!

I don't know about you, but whatever doubts I had in God up to that time were erased permanently. No matter what, I know that God has His hands covering and sheltering me from the storms of life and I pray that anyone reading this will know that God stands up, even when we have no idea that He is.

Mary Lindsey
aumal@leldc.com

Action Plan

Spend some time in prayer and communion with God. Ask Him to confirm within your spirit that the direction you are going is where He wants you to go. You must block out the external noises so you can hear from God.

Once confirmed, write down how you will water and nourish this area of your life on a daily basis.

_____

_____

_____

_____

_____

_____

_____

_____

_____

_____

_____

_____

_____

_____

_____

_____

_____

PRAY THROUGH THE FEAR

Scripture

"Have I not commanded you? Be strong and courageous. Do not be afraid; do not be discouraged, for the Lord your God will be with you wherever you go." Joshua 1:9

Lesson

There is nothing like that peace, the sweet peace that only can come from God. That is what prayer can do for you. When you pray over your fears and anxieties and truly lay them at the altar, it allows the magnificent peace that God has promised, to be manifested in your life. Doesn't that sound wonderful? Wouldn't you like to have such peace? This is not some fairytale wish. This is promised from the God who is waiting for you to call out to Him in prayer. Jeremiah 29:12,13 (NIV) says, *"Then you will call on me and come and pray to me, and I will listen to you. You will seek me and find me when you seek me with all your heart."* As well, *"the peace of God, which passeth all understanding, shall keep your hearts and minds through Christ Jesus"* (Philippians 4:7, NIV).

When you remain in constant prayer with your Heavenly Father, here are a few things that the Bible says you would be able to overcome and withstand, as well as how you will be able to handle those fears that come your way.

- Psalm 112:7-8 - *"They will have no fear of bad news; their hearts are steadfast, trusting in the Lord. Their hearts are secure, they will have no fear; in the end they will look in triumph on their foes."*

- Proverbs 29:25 - *"Fear of man will prove to be a snare, but whoever trusts in the Lord is kept safe."*

- Luke 12:32 - *"Do not be afraid, little flock, for your Father has been pleased to give you the kingdom."*

- Psalm 145:18-19 - *"The eyes of the LORD watch over those who do right; his ears are open to their cries for help. The LORD hears his people when they call to him for help. He rescues them from all their troubles."*

- Psalm 34:15, 17 - *The LORD says, "I will rescue those who love me. I will protect those who trust in my name. When they call on me, I will answer; I will be with them in trouble. I will rescue them and honor them. I will satisfy them with a long life and give them my salvation."*

Aren't the promises from God refreshing and reassuring? They truly are. However, perhaps you have been praying to God for something and He just doesn't seem to be answering. Don't lose heart. We live in a microwave society where we expect everything instantaneously but God tells us to endure even in prayer. Keep reaching out to God. Jesus illustrated this in Luke 8:1-8 (NIV), when He told the parable of the persistent widow as an example for us to persevere in prayer. It takes faith to do what the widow did but that is what God expects from you and I. Just as the judge rendered a good decision in the end, so will your Heavenly Father answer with the perfect answer for you. Pray on!

Prayer

Father, You said in Your word to ask, seek, and knock. I come before You today Lord, doing just that. First Lord, take my life as I consecrate it to You. Then Lord, take my situation and deliver me from it dear God. Tear down the strongholds Father. I will not give up, I will not let You go Lord until You bless me. I know that there is victory in Jesus, so in Jesus I put my trust. When there seems to be no hope, help me to stand on holy ground; help me to remain in constant prayer. Pray without ceasing is what I will do and I know in Your time, You will send the answer. Bless me indeed Father. In the name of Your son, Jesus Christ. Amen!

Testimony – Ericka Richardson

I thought everything would work out just fine. The kids were each four grades apart, so I would be able to save a little portion of my County Government check to send the kids to college.

My reality check came while my oldest son was in 8th grade. His report card was far from good, but I knew he was doing almost his best in school. As much as I stressed and pushed, Andre's grades barely moved up. It was time to sit down and think long and hard. Briana was a great student, but what if her grades started slipping? I decided my kids did not understand life's consequences.

That day, after a long prayer and tears, I decided to put in my notice and pursue truck driving as my new career. I made a five-year plan and put it into action. I figured it was long enough for me to learn the ropes and get my income where I needed it to be.

My family and friends thought I was crazy! *"You mean you're going to quit your good county position to do a man's job?"*

The goal was to be able to give my kids the best education and be able to send them to the college they wanted to go to, not the college I could afford. And mission accomplished! The move paid off. Our company earns well into six-figures each year and 12+ years later, we are still rolling!

Andre ended up graduating from Nassau

Community College in Long Island, NY. He is now a partner in a thriving clothing company and doing great things! Amen!

Ericka Richardson
www.coachericka.com
coacherickaonline@gmail.com

Action Plan

Choose a trusted man or woman of God and ask them to help you petition God for the situation you are facing. Then choose someone who you know is going through their own situation and pray for them daily. Remember to pray scriptures. There is nothing more rewarding than praying for someone and seeing positive change unfold in their lives. Try it!

_____

_____

_____

_____

_____

_____

_____

_____

_____

_____

_____

PUSH PAST THE FEAR

Scripture

"David also said to Solomon his son, "Be strong and courageous, and do the work. Do not be afraid or discouraged, for the LORD God, my God, is with you. He will not fail you or forsake you until all the work for the service of the temple of the LORD is finished."
1 Chronicles 28:20

Lesson

Sometimes in life we are thrown some definite curve balls, some that just seem too hard to bear. As I was completing my original manuscript, my church family tragically lost a daughter, a sister, a cousin, a friend. How do you push when someone near and dear to you is snatched away from you in an instant? How do you tell a family that it will be okay, that God does not give more than you can bear? How do you tell them to push past the pain, to push past such a tough and agonizing situation in their lives?

When your heart is aching and fear rises up within you in the form of questions like, *How can I go on without her? How can I live? Will I be able to smile again?, i*t is in these types of situations that our faith is tested. It is in these types of circumstances that you have to reach into the depths of your soul and pull out that faith that will allow you to endure. It is during these times that you have to lean on the everlasting arms of God. Turn to God and you can count on Him to step right in. Turn to His word. God's word says weeping may endure for a night but joy comes in the morning. It also says that the Holy Spirit is our Comforter and will abide with us forever. Lean on the Holy Spirit to be comforted. Matthew 5:4 says, *"Blessed are they that mourn, for they shall be comforted."*

Where do we find the strength with which to push? In God. My God, your God, our God knows these situations would happen in this sinful world and He has already made provision for us.

He walked through similar situations with others so they could help to get you through your current plight. 2 Corinthians 1:3-4 (NIV) says, *"Praise be to the God and Father of our Lord Jesus Christ, the Father of compassion and the God of all comfort, who comforts us in all our troubles, so that we can comfort those in any trouble with the comfort we ourselves receive from God."*

He understood our spirits would be crushed and is ever near to comfort. Psalm 34:18, (NIV) *"The Lord is close to the brokenhearted and saves those who are crushed in spirit." And Psalm 23:4 (NIV) "Even though I walk through the darkest valley, I will fear no evil, for you are with me; your rod and your staff, they comfort me."*

He promised these situations will not overpower us

if we put our trust in Him, who is always by our side. Isaiah 43:2, (NIV) tells us, *"When you pass through the waters, I will be with you; and when you pass through the rivers, they will not sweep over you. When you walk through the fire, you will not be burned; the flames will not set you ablaze."*

God assures us that it will not always be dark. In Psalm 18:28 (NIV), David acknowledged, *"You, Lord, keep my lamp burning; my God turns my darkness into light."* He pledged that a day is coming, when we will not have to deal with these heartaches and pains anymore. Revelation 21:4 (NIV) states, *"He will wipe every tear from their eyes. There will be no more death or mourning or crying or pain, for the old order of things has passed away."*

He gave us the blessed hope that we would be encouraged. 1 Thessalonians 4:13-18, (NIV) says, *"Brothers and sisters, we do not want you to be uninformed about those who sleep in death, so that you do not grieve like the rest of mankind, who have no hope. For we believe that Jesus died and rose again, and so we believe that God will bring with Jesus those who have fallen asleep in him. According to the Lord's word, we tell you that we who are still alive, who are left until the coming of the Lord, will certainly not precede those who have fallen asleep. For the Lord himself will come down from heaven, with a loud command, with the voice of the archangel and with the trumpet call of God, and the dead in Christ will rise first. After that, we who are still alive and are left will be caught up together with them in the clouds to meet the Lord in the air. And so we will be with the Lord forever. Therefore encourage one another with these words."*

Let's take a quick look at Job's story. Job lost all his possessions and all his 10 children. Job did nothing wrong. As a matter of fact the Bible said that he was blameless and upright, one who feared God and shunned evil. Job's story was a story of test and testimony. Job chose to push past the fear, the pain, and anguish and remain faithful to God. Though his wife asked him to curse God and die because he was in so much pain, though his friends accused him of doing wrong to cause this affliction, Job chose to heed the Lord's command and pray for them. Because Job prayed for his friends, God restored his losses doubly, including his children. And Job was able to live to see his children and grandchildren, (see Job 42:8-17). Job's abundant blessing came when he took the focus off of himself and prayed for his friends. Try finding someone to pray for and with, as they go through your tragedy with you, or their own dreadful circumstance. You will receive great peace and be blessed for it.

God is a great God. He filled scripture with the exact answers we would need to our difficult life challenges. When things seem so dark, all you have to do is look to Jesus, who is the light of the world. He will see you through and help you in your push.

Prayer

Father life seems gray right now and I do not have the strength. I feel weak, worn and battered. I am numb. I do not know how to go on. I do not know where else to turn and so I am turning to You Lord. You promised to be my Comforter. Father, I need a Comforter right now. Please heal my aching heart and ease the pain. Help me to hold on to You through my difficulties. Help me to focus on others instead of myself at this time. God I look forward to the day when there will be no more sorrows and I thank You for the blessed hope that I will see my loved one again. Until then give me peace. In Jesus' name. Amen!

Testimony – Kelli Claypool

At 3:03 a.m. on March 19, 2015, my loving husband took his last breath in my arms on the floor in our bedroom. He fought hard to overcome liver cancer but finally succumbed to the disease. In this moment, fear and panic fell upon me as I continued to hold his lifeless body close to me. I screamed out, *"Cancer, I hate you!"* as my tears fell upon his face. Since losing my soul mate, my life has been topsy-turvy. There were times during the grief process I could not get out of bed. I was paralyzed for weeks. This is when the enemy began his attacks on my mind and emotions. I was weak, tired, and vulnerable. Satan took advantage of my weakened state and tempted me with thoughts of suicide. In my deepest darkest being, I didn't want to live. I missed my husband so much. I longed to be with him, and felt life was no longer worth living. I had lost all hope.

Fear and anxiety make you lose sight of what's in front of you. The offspring of fear is hopelessness. When you have no hope, you're being influenced by a lie. The Biblical definition of hope is a "joyful anticipation of breakthrough." Zechariah 9:12 says, *"Return to the stronghold [of security], you prisoners of hope; even today do I declare that I will restore double your former prosperity to you."*

If hope is the joyful anticipation of breakthrough and the Lord promises us He will restore double, then I believe we are to praise Him - as this is where strength is found. If this is true, then as we praise Him, we gain strength through our breakthrough, and that is where we find hope!

2 Timothy 1:7 says, *"For God has not given us the spirit of fear; but of power, and of love, and of a sound mind."* Having a sound mind is critical as it explores what God says is true. Colossians 3:2 says, *"Keep your minds on things that are above, not on things that are on the earth."* Every area of your life God touches, comes into fullness and you never think the same way about this area again. If you keep your mind on Kingdom thoughts, your fear, anxiety, and

hopelessness becomes hopeful, and this is where breakthrough begins.

While I continue to have days of sadness and loneliness, I will not allow myself to be overcome by a spirit of fear. Jeremiah 29:11 says, *"For I know the plans I have for you, declares the Lord, plans for welfare and not for evil, to give you a future and a hope.*

When we don't give up, that's when our trust [our faith] is fortified and hope abounds. Be encouraged today!

Kelli Claypool
www.divatalkradio.com
kelli@divatalkradio.com

Action Plan
Continue to reflect on the scriptures provided, pray, and journal your thoughts. Always reach out to someone for help, especially someone whom God has brought through a similar situation. Your blessing is on the way.

_____

_____

_____

_____

_____

_____

SING THROUGH THE FEAR

Scripture
"O Zion, that bringest good tidings, get thee up into the high mountain; O Jerusalem, that bringest good tidings, lift up thy voice with strength; lift it up, be not afraid; say unto the cities of Judah, Behold your God!" Isaiah 40:9

Lesson

There is nothing more calming, soothing, uplifting, and refreshing than a beautiful song. When I was growing up, one of the youth groups I was a member of had a law that ended in *"Keep a song in my heart; Go on God's errands."* That has stuck with me. In order to move forward in God's calling; in order to get up out of your dark place and forge ahead in God's purpose for your life, it's important to have a song in your heart. This means you should be "cheerful, happy and let the influence of your life be a sunshine to others."[3] You see, in life, what you do affects others. How you react to situations is crucial to others who are watching you.

The Bible tells us in Psalm 100, *"Make a joyful noise unto the Lord, all ye lands. Serve the Lord with gladness: come before his presence with singing. Know ye that the Lord he is God: it is he that hath made us, and not we ourselves; we are his people, and the sheep of his pasture. Enter into his gates with thanksgiving, and into his courts with praise: be thankful unto him, and bless his name. For the Lord is good; his mercy is everlasting; and his truth endureth to all generations."* When you know about the goodness of the Lord, how can you keep quiet? How can you be afraid to sing His praises? How can you not lift up your voice and sing? Not everyone is given the gift of singing but sing anyway. Sing in your shower; sing in your home.

Then for those who have been blessed with a beautiful voice but are fearful of shining for Jesus, I have a message for you. Think about the parable of the talents in Matthew 25:14-30. God entrusted you with the talent of singing. Will you use it and multiply it or will you hide it? Would you prefer to hear, *"Well done, good and faithful servant. You have been faithful over a little; I will set you over much. Enter into the joy of your master"* (Matthew 25:23, ESV). Or will you prefer to have your talent taken from you and given to others who will use it? Your talent is not just for you, it's for bringing glory to God and for uplifting others. Do not let fear hold you back. Sing through the fears.

Prayer

Father, today I choose to sing. Lord, show me what Your plan is for my life, whether it's just to sing in my home, in the shower, or locally at my church, or whether You intend for me to reach a larger audience with the voice that You have given me. Help me to follow Your leading and sing to Your glory. In Jesus' name. Amen!

Testimony – Debbie Brinkley

Matthew 5:4-10 (MSG) *"You're blessed when you've worked and you feel you've lost what is most dear to you, only then can you be embraced by the one most dear to you. You're blessed when you are content with who you are no more no less. This is the moment you find yourself proud owners of everything that can't be bought. You're blessed when you've worked up a good appetite for God; he's food and drink in the best meal you'll ever eat. You're blessed when you care. At the moment of being careful you find yourself cared for. You're blessed when you get your inside world, your mind and heart put right. Then you can see God in the outside world. You're blessed when you can show people how to cooperate instead of compete and fight. That's when you discover who you really are, and your place in God's family. You're blessed when your commitment to God provokes persecution. The persecution drives you deeper into God's kingdom."*

God wants to crown your life with His goodness.

2015 was one of the worst years of my life. I would have lost my mind if it had not been for the Lord who was on my side. It was in this place the Holy Spirit gave me songs in the midnight hour. Jesus would meet me in the darkest hours between midnight and 3 am. I would sing the songs that had been placed in my spirit to help me make it through the night. I heard some say the darkest hour is just before dawn. It was during these hours the devil would show up and try to tell me to give up and throw in the towel. It was in those hours I would ball up my hand and hold on to Gods unchanging hand and sing some of the songs my mama used to sing.

As I look back, I understood what my mama was doing all those times I heard her walking through the house singing songs of praise unto God. I have faced many adversities in my life. I too have learned to keep a song of praise in my mouth. It was those songs of praise that kept me when I thought I wouldn't make it through the night. I would lay in my bed with tears streaming down my face singing praises unto God. It was in this place my mama's God became my God.

I could feel His presence in the still hours of the night. He was letting me know He would never leave me nor forsake me. I needed to be still and know He is God. It was during these times He would remind me of where He has brought me from. All He required from me was to let go. Let go of the things I held dear to me, the marriage, businesses, houses, and the cars. All of the things I thought made me, me. This "me" is what God wanted to get rid of because I kept getting in the way of what He was trying to do. After I walked away from everything I held on to, it was there I began to realize God was only trying to get me to give up those things so that He could give me something better. Some of those things I had been praying for, I was afraid to leave my comfort zone to get. At the end of the day none of it matters if I don't have Him. Matthew 6:33 states, *"Seek ye first the kingdom of God and all his righteousness then all of these things shall be added unto you."* As I look back over 2015 and all the things I had to go through to get here, I can say if it had not been for the Lord on my side I don't know where I would be. Never give up even when you feel like the answer to your prayers are a billion miles away. Keep a song in your mouth and Jesus will carry you through.

Debbie Brinkley
Mzdebbie59@yahoo.com

Action Plan

Surround yourself with music. Listen to at least one uplifting song each day. Keep that song in your heart.

For the singers, make a pledge today to use your talent for the Lord to bless others.

SHARE THROUGH THE FEAR

Scripture

"Do not be afraid; you will not be put to shame. Do not fear disgrace; you will not be humiliated. You will forget the shame of your youth and remember no more the reproach of your widowhood." Isaiah 54:4

Lesson

Oftentimes when we go through situations in life, we tend to keep it a secret even when we've seen the miraculous hand of God in those situations. Imagine if the Bible did not capture the story of Job, Hannah, Joseph, Moses and the Israelites, or David. Do you realize what a blessing these stories have been throughout history? Do you realize that many would have been lost had it not been for these stories? Well the same holds true for your story. There is strength in your story. Don't be afraid to share it.

Share how God has brought you through so someone can learn from it.

- Whether the doctors gave you six months to live and you are still here after two years;
- Whether you were infertile and God blessed you with a child;
- Whether you were thrown in prison falsely or otherwise and God brought you out to a victorious life;

- Whether you were headed down a wrong path and God allowed a situation to happen that turned you right around toward the life of your calling and purpose;
- Whether you faced a seemingly impossible situation with the walls closing in around you and God in a miraculous way opened the way of escape; or
- Whether others see only the bad that you do but God has shown you over and over again, because of your relationship with Him and your continued renewing of your heart to Him that He loves you.

Whatever your circumstance, people need to hear your story. Don't listen to the voices of criticism and condemnation. Don't measure yourself against others. Share your story, and remember your story will not be as effective if you choose to only focus on the parts that are safe, clean and acceptable to others. Look at David. He was an adulterer and a murderer, among other things, yet he humbled himself, repented and was called a man after God's own heart. Imagine again if his story was left out of the Bible. Your story should not be left out of the books of history. Through your honest sharing, you show God as loving and caring, and a God who can do the impossible. You can only do this when you focus on God as your only audience and shut out the voices of fear and doubt.

When you share your story a miracle happens. It

will give others hope to press through their current situation, knowing a brighter day is coming. It will help others to understand God is a faithful God. It will show others the delivering power of your God. It will help others break free from their bondage. It will help lift burdens. Your story is powerful. It will change lives. Share it!

Prayer

Father, I thank You for all the stories in the Bible, stories of hope, of Your provision, deliverance, forgiveness, and blessing to Your children. I thank You that we all have a story to share no matter how difficult it may be. Teach me to let go of any fear of what others will think and focus on You and the hope that my story will bring to others. Help me Lord to share my story whether in song, speech, or writing so that others might be blessed by it. May all the praise and all the glory go to You in my testimony. In Jesus' name. Amen!

Testimony – Dr. Emmy Wu

In the movie The Color Purple, Oprah Winfrey's character was quoted with this now infamous line, "All my life I had to fight." This adequately describes the life I had to live. I was raised by my beautiful family. My mother had abandoned me by the time I was 2-years-old. My father raised me with the help of my grandparents, aunts, and uncles. I was a bit of a sheltered child. I had other siblings by my mom, with different dads, but I only considered them stepbrothers and sisters. I was my father's only child. My father worked very hard to provide for me. Yet, I found myself being lonely and because my dad had no other daughters, all of my friends were boys. I was a "tom boy" of sorts.

At eight years old I started experimenting with magic. One of the first items I received was Ouija board. When I was 11 years old, one of my male friends forced me into friend's dad's home and he raped me. I never told anyone about this. I kept this secret so deep within me out of fear. I became rebellious. I began acting out towards my father. I didn't feel good within myself; it was as if my mind was not right. Whenever my father would go to work, I would go and hang out with the older boys. I lied about my age, so they never really knew how old I was. The darkness within me was taking over. I was becoming very hateful. I never told my dad about the rape. I didn't want him hurting and I thought I would be punished.

I didn't pray as much anymore. I was going to church with my grandfather, but sometimes I just didn't feel God. I started having sex again at age 15. I became pregnant and had my son at 16-years-old. My dad was heartbroken. My dad had full custody of both my son and I, since I was a minor. I lived with my father while I finished high school, however the streets kept calling me. One night I remember coming home late from school. My dad was so angry with me, he kicked me out and I ended up staying with a friend. I left, but my dad made me leave my son. I called the police but was told I could not take him. This hurt me deeply.

In 1996 or 97, I moved to Atlanta and began modeling and singing in a girl's group. At this point, I had another son. We were preparing to audition for a major label and I asked my aunt to keep him to which she obliged, telling me, the studio was no place for my son. Now this son was gone too. Once again, I found myself torn from the inside out and began beating myself up. My life now consisted of partying and drugs. I didn't care anymore. I thought to myself, my mother was never around, so why should I be any different. I started dating drug dealers and working for them. Although, this was not the design for my life, I became numb to it all. I temporarily moved in with a pimp and began exotic dancing. I lived with him for a while, but decided to leave there and go back and live with my aunt.

In 1999, I met my last three children's father. We were together for 11 years, but these years were filled with Hell. He was very physically and sexually abusive, but I stayed with him because I wanted my family. I thought it was my fault. We eventually lost our home and were having to live in hotels. I would leave and go back. Feb 4, 2011 I knew I was getting money. I was praying that he would leave and go to work so I would have my chance of escape. This same day, I caught a train and moved back to my aunt's home. I never looked back. I wasn't sure if I had it in me to be a mother but God had a plan. Eventually, I was able to move into my own place. I began working full-time and was able to purchase a car. Yet, I still wanted to party and hang out.

March 2014, feeling something was missing, I asked a friend to please take me to church with her. On this day my life was changed. I went to church and a man walked up to me and asked if I was okay. I told him yes. He said no you're not and he handed me something and said put in my purse. At this time, I had been in a car wreck and was driving a rental. While there, a gentle man was speaking and he pulled me out of the crowd. He said to me I was crying for five years, but God said no more. Something shifted in my life at this time, I went to the car and looked in my purse, therein was the money given to me by the gentleman. He and his wife took me in as part of their family, blessed me with a truck, and loved me as if we were blood related. I never knew anyone else could love me like family. I should have been dead four years before at the hands of a man or in the car wreck, but I realized God put a fight in me, a fight for my freedom and my life. No matter what you are going through – fight, for yourself, for your children, for your life. In the midst of my suffering, I went through my personal death, burial, and resurrection, just like God, our Father. I needed to see my true reflection as God sees me. Know that you are not a mistake. I finally gained myself. I am now a self-relationship flow coach and an ordained minister/prophetess. God is always with us and He is there in the storm. I fought through my storm and I am encouraging you to fight as well. You're not alone. Let God fight with you and for you. I would not be the woman I am right now without every situation that happened in my past and without that will to fight. You too can have the life you want and deserve.

Dr. Emmy Wu
veganchefemmywu@gmail.com

Action Plan

Reflect on your struggles of the past. Start documenting how you got through those situations. Recognize God's hand in those instances and start journaling your story. Pray and ask God how He wants you to share it.

_____

_____

_____

THINK ABOVE THE FEAR

Scripture

"Hearken unto me, ye that know righteousness, the people in whose heart is my law; fear ye not the reproach of men, neither be ye afraid of their revilings." Isaiah 51:7

Lesson

In a motivational video created for his followers, Darren Hardy asked them to imagine their mind as an empty glass. The glass would only hold what they put in it. If they fed their minds with dark, negative, dirty, fearsome, worrisome content this is exactly how they would see the world. His message to the audience was that in order to think positive, in order for the content in the glass to be clear again, they must flush it with clean, clear water. They must flush their brain with positive content and thoughts based on what they watch, what they listen to, and what they read.

I remember a song when I was growing up that I now teach my children, "Watch your eyes, watch your eyes what they see; For your Father up above is looking down in love; watch your eyes, watch your eyes what they see." The song continued with watch your ears, watch your ears what they hear; watch your mouth, watch your mouth what you speak; watch your feet, watch your feet where they go. In order to think positive thoughts, you have to filter what goes into your brain, you have to get rid of the negative influences and shut out the naysayers.

Let's revisit the story of Job. His story is a testimony of true faith in the midst of tribulation and not allowing negative influences to determine your thoughts and actions. Similar to the negativity imposed on Job from his wife, you are going to face negative influences from the outside, telling you to give up on God when you know God is awesome. Imagine if Job had listened to his wife telling him to curse God and die. He would have missed out on so much. Look at the abundance he was blessed with after he went through this situation. Think about the entire scenario. God allowed that to happen to him because He wanted it to be a message, not only to Job, but for all of humanity to be able to look at this story and recognize that someone went through all of this hardship and still came out victorious.

Regardless of what you are going through, think positive thoughts. Remember Job's story, his triumph, and how God multiplied Job's possessions and gave him back his children. They may not have been his original children but God gave him a family he could love, share his experience with and enjoy. This is why I am encouraging you to stand strong, so you can have a story to share that will be a blessing to others.

Don't forget God said He will not give you more than you can bear. You have to dig deep in your soul and find this belief. You have to believe God will not give you more than you can bear, and if He has given it to you, you can handle it. Don't try to do it on your own. Remember the Bible says, *"I can do all things through Christ who strengthens me"* (Philippians 4:13 NKJV). Reach out to God for this strength. Speak to Him. Listen for His voice, direction, and leading.

It's all in the thought process. Think positive. Think God loves me and is with me. Think I can do all things. Think God will help me. Think your fear away.

Prayer

Father, I thank You for Your word which tells me I am more than a conqueror and I can do all things through Christ who gives me strength. Help me to continue to fill my mind with these positive scriptures of hope. Lord, for the years of negativity that has made its way into my mind, help me to flush it out by filling it with positive thoughts, as I read Your word and other positive and inspiring material. Thank You for the power of transformation and for knowing and understanding my past does not define me. You are a God who heals the broken hearted and binds up their wounds. I pray today that You bind up the wounds of negativity in my life and renew my mind in You. Father I choose to think about Your love and Your goodness in my life. Thank You Lord for Your mercies. In Jesus' name. Amen!

Testimony – Cherese Spand

Prior to the realization of my fears, my entire life felt stuck. I have an intense passion to educate, nurture, and support people, giving them hope and vision. My spirit was crying out to do so in a greater and more effective way.

I prayed and asked for guidance then boom! A Facebook friend posted she was starting a coaching session, and it has been a phenomenal experience.

My view of my life has changed dramatically since participating. Fear had me in bondage from many different areas in my life. My assignment was to write out what beliefs gripped me in fear, and, why I had an issue facing these fears. As I wrote the fears out and began to focus on what I wanted, my old belief system was being eliminated. My DNA had to be reprogrammed. It's like ask and you shall receive. Your life starts to completely transition, as thoughts and visions become clearer. Prior to retraining and overcoming my mind was filled with doubt and hesitation, always wondering if I was worthy and deserving of a fantastic life, in addition to a fabulous career.

Since learning these principles and concepts, my business went through a great transition. We have grown from a team of one to a team of more than 40 within a few months and now expanding into the Tri-State. We are on track to change hundreds and thousands of lives. I am forever grateful I came to the realization of and faced those fears, and as a bonus, I have forged new friendships and business partners as well.

Whatever it takes to get rid of the False Expectations Appearing Real aka fear, just do it. The results will be rewarding. You will have to put in the work. But, if you have the courage to believe that you are worthy, then you shall receive everything in store for you.

Cherese Spand
Clslifestyle1@gmail.com

Action Plan

Start a routine of reading one passage of scripture every day and meditate on that Scripture throughout each day. Perhaps invest in a scripture promise box. Watch the manifestation of God in your life as you focus on His word.

_____

_____

_____

_____

_____

_____

_____

_____

LOVE OVER THE FEAR

Scripture
"You who bring good news to Zion, go up on a high mountain. You who bring good news to Jerusalem, lift up your voice with a shout, lift it up, do not be afraid; say to the towns of Judah, "Here is your God!" Isaiah 40:9

Lesson

The Bible tells us in John 10:10, *"the thief comes only to steal, kill and destroy but God has come that we might have life, and have it more abundantly."* Do you realize that the thief does not show up the same way all the time and that sometimes he comes in the form of fear and insecurity? It could be regarding your marriage, finances, future, or even how people perceive you. When these thoughts overtake you, you could feel in utter turmoil. Remember God did not give you a spirit of fear, but of power and love and of a sound mind (2 Timothy 1:7). All those negative feelings are of the enemy, the thief, who wants to destroy your spirit.

The best remedy for these fears and insecurities is love. 1 John 4:18 declares, *"There is no fear in Love. Perfect love casteth out fear."* The love being referred to here is found in God because God is love. God's love can help you face situations you are afraid of in your life. You have to trust God and abide in His love to help you let go of your insecurities. The best way to recognize God's love in your life is to record it, not just in your mind because you may forget, but on paper, perhaps in a journal. If you don't know where the rent money is going to come from and at the 11th hour you receive it, write it in your journal. If someone shows you kindness, write it down. If you receive a new customer, journal this as well. You will be surprised at the many blessings (love) that's bestowed upon you as God's child. It's the little things in life that matter most and we tend to overlook them.

Don't allow anything, fear, doubt, or insecurity, to separate you from the love of God. Here's what the Bible says in Romans 8:38 – 39. *"For I am convinced that neither death nor life, neither angels nor demons, neither the present nor the future, nor any powers, neither height nor depth, nor anything else in all creation, will be able to separate us from the love of God that is in Christ Jesus our Lord."* God loves you and wants the best for you. He said He will not hold back any good gift from you. Therefore, whatever you need in accordance with His good will for your life, be it financial, emotional, physical, or spiritual, He will provide.

"Whoever does not love does not know God, because God is love" (1John 4:8, NIV). Once you are convinced of and receive God's love in your life, it becomes time to share this love with others. Just as

God's love transforms you, it is the same way your love will make a difference in someone else's life. I love a quote that I read from motivational speaker Tony Robbins who said, *"Cultivate the emotions of love and warmth. If someone comes to you in a state of hurt or anger, and you consistently respond with love and warmth, eventually that person's state will change and his or her intensity will melt away."* Wouldn't it be wonderful to know that because of your love and efforts, lives have been changed? Love is what you are called to do.

Prayer

Father, thank You for loving me with an everlasting love, a love that cannot be broken, a love that's strong enough to cast out all fears. Dear God, help me to accept Your love in my life, knowing it is freely given to me. Whenever the feelings of doubt and insecurities come upon me, I will confess Your love for me. Lord, I am determined not to let anything separate me from Your love and I know as long as I keep this determination I will have victory. Please help me to show love to others as well so that they too can understand the power of love and come to know You God, who is love. Thank You Father, in the name of Jesus Christ. Amen!

Testimony – Mary Williams

I was a young army wife in Darmstadt, Germany. My husband and I had been married for about two years and decided to try for our first baby. We became pregnant right away, but a couple months into the pregnancy, I miscarried. We were devastated, but we knew God had a plan for our family. Not too long after the miscarriage, I remember calling my mom and telling her I was pregnant again. I didn't hear the enthusiasm in her voice that I had heard before. I now realize, as much as I had a desire to become a mother and have a baby, she had just as strong of a desire as a mother to protect her baby - me. She asked me if it was too soon after the miscarriage to get pregnant again. At the time, I could not tell her I had to try again, as soon as possible after the miscarriage. If I didn't, I was afraid I would become paralyzed with fear and never try to have a child, again. Needless to say, my husband was ecstatic, we were having a boy and he would have a junior. It was a good pregnancy without complication.

At 36 weeks, we discovered there was no heartbeat. My beloved son died in utero. I was induced into labor and gave birth to him within 48 hours of the induction. Our hearts were broken. The pain and emptiness almost consumed us. We got to hold our dear Cory in our arms and kiss his little sweet face, before saying our final goodbye. It was in this moment God promised me He would bless us with a son.

A couple of years later, I gave birth to my oldest daughter and four years after this I had my second daughter. However, between the births of my two daughters, I had another miscarriage. By this time, my husband and I had developed a true relationship with the Lord. We knew everything happened for a reason. We were grateful to have two beautiful healthy daughters. We were getting older and decided this was it for children. I still remembered the promised God had made us.

Fourteen years after the birth and death of my son, we decided to give it one more try. Despite the fact we both were over 35 (which was considered a high-risk pregnancy due to my age) and my husband had had a vasectomy (which we were able to get reversed, but was told it would take a while before we conceived, if at all), we had a son, Damon Jr. He is a healthy, adventurous, funny, talented, smart 8- year-old that has brought more joy to our family than we could have ever imagined.

God honors His promises and His word, it will not return to Him void. We trusted God where we could not trace Him and He blessed in abundance.

Mary Williams
perrlsofwellness@gmail.com

Action Plan

1. Think about the good things God has done in your life in the past month. No matter how small they were, journal them. Thank Him for His love. Keep doing this going forward.

2. Think of one act of kindness you can do for someone and do it in the next day or two. Journal how it made you feel.

_____

_____

_____

_____

_____

_____

_____

_____

_____

_____

_____

_____

_____

_____

_____

_____

_____

_____

RISE ABOVE THE FEAR

Scripture
"And say unto him, Take heed, and be quiet; fear not, neither be fainthearted for the two tails of these smoking firebrands, for the fierce anger of Rezin with Syria, and of the son of Remaliah." Isaiah 7:4

Lesson

Do you know you have the power within you to rise above all your fears and concerns? Yes you do. God's word says in 2 Timothy 1:7 (NKJV) that He *"(God) has not given you a spirit of fear, but of POWER and love and of a sound mind."* Therefore don't let your fears keep you from what you want in life. You have been given the power by God to rise above them. Make your dream list a priority over your fears.

I know it can be hard to see forward when you are so blinded with the trials and struggles of life. Why not take God's word literally? Do you want to see more clearly? Then focus on Revelation 3:18 which says, *"I counsel you to buy from me gold refined in the fire, so you can become rich; and white clothes to wear, so you can cover your shameful nakedness; and salve to put on your eyes, so you can see."* God is the only one who can make the dark areas in your life bright again.

God knows the end from the beginning and

therefore your life's pages are already written in God's book. You have a choice, to stay stuck on the page you are on or move forward to the next page. Do not give up and do not give in. Do not stop on the page of disappointment and discouragement. Trust God. Keep pressing on. Rise above the pain, hurt, brokenness, and the wounds. Rise up against the heaviness you feel, the loneliness you experience, the weariness in your body, and the tears you have cried. God will see you through. When you get tired, discouraged, and frustrated, focus on God. Do not try to understand what He does or what He does not do, but rather focus on who He is. That's what would give you the strength to rise above all those negative feelings.

What if you thought about who you would inspire rather than what you can accomplish? Do you think that would help you rise and move forward? Focus on the lives you can touch or the lives you would have neglected to touch, if you refused to rise above your fears. I'm sure you don't want that burden on your hands. Remember, you have a responsibility to live a life that brings joy to yourself and to others as well. Too many people allow the fear of failure to keep them from moving forward in the work God has called them to. Don't be one of those people. There is greatness in you. Claim it and move towards it. Be someone's hero. God will strengthen you and help you as you RISE.

Prayer

Father, thank You for words of encouragement that You provide through scripture and through Your people. Help me to focus more on the outcome rather than the current stresses. Place Your love in my heart, so I can impart it unto others through the steps I take to move forward in Your calling. Help me to realize that there are those who are looking at me and that the things I do and do not do, will impact their lives for the Kingdom. I admit Lord, this is a responsibility that sometimes is overwhelming, but You are able to keep me and to sustain me. Therefore, today I choose to rise above all the fears and be a light to Your people. In Jesus' name. Amen!

Testimony – Traci Henderson-Smith

Fear doesn't always appear as a gripping sense of dread or an overwhelming concern of something unwelcomed occurring. Sometimes it is an undercurrent, subtle and unassuming. An inconspicuous stream flowing beneath the perfect performance, job well done, or selfless show of support or act of sacrifice. Sometimes fear shows up as avoidance.

Avoidance is perhaps the least detectable fear. Others can identify it, but the person it possesses has a more difficult time seeing it within him or herself. Shrouded by what appears as legitimate excuses: when would I find the time, maybe when I've saved enough money, one dream at a time—I'm supporting [insert name or role here] right now, when the children are older, I have enormous responsibilities at work and a lot of people depend upon me, and the list goes on. Fear by way of avoidance is stealth-like and a killer of dreams. It resides in the subconscious planted by a person or incident that has marked you. It is in direct opposition with how you were created. It opposes who you would be and the choices you would make if this voice, image, or idea competing with who you really are had not been introduced.

The aim of this competitor—this enemy, is to make you think being great is so improbable; you never receive it as your expected end. You put off or avoid giving weight to nurturing, cultivating, and harvesting the true beauty buried within your gift, talent, anointing, or purpose. You pour out your awesomeness, as many have no doubt called it, upon everything and everyone else. You are not without accomplishment. As a great parent, supportive spouse, inspiring teacher, top employee, mentor, coach, or minister, you shine. Others call upon you to give more of yourself to them, their visions, and goals. You are in high demand, the one to have on any team and would most likely find the question, *What are you afraid of?* offensive. *What am I afraid of? Do you not see me ruling in my world?"* would most likely be the response. Are you however, in fact ruling, dominating deep within yourself? Is there a book, play, movie, song, position, business, invention, platform, or mountain, you've dreamed of mastering? Why haven't you stepped to it? Why haven't you done it? Running beneath your selflessness is a still quiet stream of avoidance—fear. What are you afraid of? Why won't you decide to be great for you? We have to be willing to ask ourselves these questions and get honest about what we uncover.

What we do, is most times centered on or is designed for others and there is nothing wrong with this. However, what we *do* is not who we *are*. Who we are is solely about ourselves. We were taught somewhere not to be 'all about ourselves.' It is selfish. We never gave ourselves permission to conquer both. We became masters at shelving our dreams, squashing our desires, and placing on the backburner what we'd like to accomplish in this life for our own satisfaction. I did. Entertainment writer, business owner, supportive wife, award-winning director of programs, mentor, motivator, writer and developer of children's curriculum and still hadn't gotten to me. It is hard to sift through that and come up unfulfilled. It is even harder to admit it.

In 2002, Dr. Myles Monroe, standing in my restaurant, said to me, *"The love and passion in me, excellence, and the best of what I am shows in everything I touch.*" He challenged me not to die empty, not let the grave get my gifts and talents. He said to do all I was created for. It was not until his premature death in 2014, I realized I had not taken on his challenge. I made a promise. The grave would not get what I was created for. I dared to dream again and see myself doing the impossible. I chose to rise above the avoidance, stop masking, and be unafraid to selfishly and unapologetically pour as much into myself as I have into others. I understand what God put in me; He expects to get out of me. I now live a life dedicated to doing, having, and being everything God ever said concerning me.

Traci Henderson Smith
thswritingwell@gmail.com

Action Plan

Martin Luther once said, *"An individual has not started living until he can rise above the narrow confines of his individualistic concerns to the broader concerns of all humanity."* Create a vision board of what the outcome would look like if you took the steps to RISE as we discussed in the lesson. Celebrate the end result as you thank God in advance for taking you through the journey.

_____

_____

WALK THROUGH THE FEAR

Scripture

"Do not fear, for you will not be ashamed; Neither be disgraced, for you will not be put to shame; For you will forget the shame of your youth, And will not remember the reproach of your widowhood anymore." Isaiah 54:4

Lesson

Our faith is tested in many ways. One of those ways is with infertility. I included this topic because of my own struggles and triumph in this area of my life. I am eternally grateful to God for taking me through my faith journey, which resulted in the most precious gifts I ever received, my two sons.

God instructed us to be fruitful and multiply and so most women dream of being a mother. Being diagnosed with infertility is a true test of faith but like with all tests, you must stand. When your faith is nowhere in sight, when you just can't seem to find the strength, when all you see is your fear of not having a child; climb up your mind's eye. Climb up to a high point; into a tree; climb up the mountaintop and look ahead. Look ahead and you will see faith. Read the Word of God to strengthen your faith. Then you will be able to walk the walk of faith. *"Blessed is she who has believed that the Lord would fulfill his promises to her!"* (Luke 1:45, NIV).

Isaiah 54 (NKJV) starts with God saying in verses 1-3, *"'Sing, O barren, You who have not borne! Break forth into singing, and cry aloud, You who have not labored with child! For more are the children of the desolate than the children of the married woman,' says the Lord. 'Enlarge the place of your tent, And let them stretch out the curtains of your dwellings; Do not spare; Lengthen your cords, And strengthen your stakes. For you shall expand to the right and to the left, And your descendants will inherit the nations, And make the desolate cities inhabited.'"*

If you are going through infertility issues or you know someone who is, remember all things are possible with God. God said sing, cry aloud, and enlarge the place of your tent. Enlarge your tent by believing and embracing God's promises. That belief will bring you peace. Oh yes, doubt will kick back in from time to time but you have to find your way back to that place of peace. Keep reading God's word and keep on believing.

Also, remember God said in His word that in all things give thanks. You are not expected to wait for the blessing to say thank you to God. You are to thank Him now. The key to this, the key to walking in faith, is staying in God's word, which is filled with His promises. Read God's word daily and speak the things He says in His word. Things like *"your descendants will inherit the nations."* Once you read God's word and believe it, then you continue to pour out your heart's desires to Him. After you do, embrace the attitude of Hannah as in 1 Samuel 1:18 (KJV), *"She went her way, ...and her countenance was no more sad."* In all things, you must trust God.

I heard a preacher say that when we go to Heaven and the books are open before us and we see why certain things happen in life, then it will be clear why God allowed the things He did. Until then, we have to keep trusting and believing. God is God all by Himself and He knows best, He wants the best for all, and He will not hold back good gifts from His children. Embrace that and be at peace as you walk the walk of faith.

Prayer

Dear God, You are an awesome wonder. You love Your children so much that You chose to make provisions in Your word to help us through each and every situation we could face. Father, I thank You for Your promises. Lord, I choose today to walk in faith believing that You have my best interest at heart and that You will not hold back any good gift from me. Help me not to give up but to hold my head high, knowing that I am a child of the King of Kings. Help me to hold on to and focus more on who You are, rather than trying to understand what You do or do not do. Father, knowing that there is nothing too hard for You, I chose to trust You today and always. In Jesus' name. Amen!

Testimony – Wanza Leftwich

When I was diagnosed with infertility several years ago, my husband and I were devastated. Like most couples, we dreamed of starting a family. After all, God instructed us to be fruitful and multiply. With the diagnosis, overwhelming fear of never being able to conceive a child crept in. I feared the worst and often asked myself many "what if" questions, including what if my husband leaves me? I spent days, weeks, months, and years with this worry and fear until I was reminded of a Bible scripture I learned years prior when I was in college which says, *"Blessed is she who has believed that the Lord would fulfill his promises to her!"* (Luke 1:45, NIV).

As I recall the passage, I recognized this was not only an assurance from God that He would fulfill His promises, but the passage specifically said, *"To her"* and this was exciting to me since most scriptures refer to "he." I knew in this moment God was speaking directly to me. I embraced this promise and moved forward with a new sense of confidence. Yes there were moments of despair and disappointment but through it all there was an overarching feeling of peace that I indeed would be a mother one day.

With this belief, I contemplated the suggestions

the doctors were making regarding In-Vitro Fertilization, but God spoke through my husband when he decided we should wait. The longer it took the more fear crept right back in until I felt I had reached a breaking point and I cried out to God saying, I cannot keep living like this. In this moment of despair, God spoke to me once again. God said, I need you to get happy now. I need you to stay away from things that keep you depressed. I need you to stop reading all those blogs on infertility. I need you to go by My Word and speak what I say in My Word. I need you to speak and live as if things are already as you desire.

With that, I disconnected myself from the fear and depression and started surrounding myself with life. I forced myself to be excited about Mother's Day. I made a conscious decision to put myself in situations and environments where people had what I wanted. I attended baby showers, children's birthday parties, and supported less fortunate children. I embraced Hannah's attitude in 1 Samuel 1:18 (KJV), *"She went her way, and her countenance was no more sad."*

Just as God showed Hannah favor, He did the same for my husband and me. Today, we are blessed with two beautiful miracle girls without fertility treatments as the doctors had envisioned. With these blessings, I published the book, *Faith and Fertility* and established my support group to help women and families with fertility issues, teaching them infertility is not the end, but the beginning of a miracle.

Wanza Leftwich

www.wanzaleftwich.com

wanzaleftwich@gmail.com

Action Plan

1. Read Genesis 18:14; Jeremiah 32:17; Jeremiah 32:27; and Luke 18:27 as you seek to strengthen your faith in God. Know that there is nothing too hard for Him.

2. Then read 1 Thessalonians 3:1-13. Write out your test and your testimony.

_____

_____

_____

_____

_____

_____

_____

_____

_____

_____

_____

_____

A Further Call To Action

I don't want this to be a book you read and just continue on with your life as usual. I want you to reflect on where you are and where God wants you to be. Be encouraged as you take action to bridge the gap. I want you to commit to begin (or continue) your journey towards Releasing the Fear and Walking in Faith. It's what I did in writing this book. Will you join me?

Ellen G. White, nee Harmon, was a perfect example of someone who would be considered inadequate to be an author or journalist. She was "not a brilliant student, nor was she, college-educated. She was not a skilled or published writer. It would be difficult to say that Ellen White's remarkable literary production was merely a product of human genius and invention. Her contemporaries, knowing her background and minimal education, also knew that something more than human wisdom was responsible for her incisive, commanding eloquence in print as well as in the pulpit.

In late spring 1845, Ellen Harmon's hand, trembling in weakness, was unable to write, but in a vision she was told to write what she saw. For the first time, her 'hand became steady.' Many years later she recalled this experience, 'The Lord has said, "Write out the things which I shall give you." I commenced when I was very young to do this work. The hand that was feeble and trembling because of infirmities became steady as soon as I took the pen in my hand, and since those first writings I have been able to write. God has given me the ability to write. . . . The right hand scarcely ever has a disagreeable sensation. It never wearies. It seldom ever trembles (1900).' By the close of her seventy-year ministry, her literary productions totaled approximately 100,000 pages, or the equivalent of 25 million words, including letters, diaries, periodical articles, pamphlets, and books.

At the time of Mrs. White's death (1915), twenty-four books were currently in print and two more were at the publishers awaiting publication. In the 1990s, 128 titles were in print bearing Ellen White's name, including books that are compilations of her thoughts on various subjects."[4]

Ellen White was a person who followed God's calling and in turn the Lord turned her negatives into positives and she became a prominent literary figure. I have recognized that the key to her success is pushing beyond her infirmities and walking the road led by her heavenly Father. This is what I have committed to.

What about you? Can you identify some examples of people who have beaten the odds and excelled in the area in which they were called? Can you identify with R.H. Macy who had seven failed businesses before finally hitting it big with Macy's? Can you identify with Oprah Winfrey who is now dubbed one of the richest and most successful women in the world and one of the most prominent faces on television, but who initially endured a rough and abusive childhood and career setbacks, such as being fired from being a television reporter because she was deemed unfit for television? Can you identify with Steve Chen, an immigrant to the United States from Taiwan, who could have used his immigrant status as excuse but instead went on to co-found YouTube? Or maybe, you can identify with Alberto Gonzalez, who dared to dream and take action, leaving his lucrative law practice in Texas to join the Bush Administration and later become the first Hispanic Attorney General?

If none of these resonate with you, why not conduct your own research and find someone to identify with. Then remind yourself that if they can do it, you can do it too because God promised to help you. Take the mental attitude of Michael Jordan, hailed as the best basketball player of all time despite being cut from his high school basketball team. You see, Michael Jordan did not allow setbacks and fears to stop him from playing the game. Instead he said, *"I have missed more than 9,000 shots in my career. I have lost almost 300 games. On 26 occasions I have been entrusted to take the game winning shot, and I missed. I have failed over and over and over again in my life. And that is why I succeed."*

Success awaits you. Believe in yourself and trust in God.

Testimony – Jessica Thompson

As I exited the doors of a world I had known for more than 15 years, I was riddled with fear.

- Fear of the unknown.
- Fear that I'd never be noticed again.
- Fear that I'd never be respected again.
- Fear that I wasn't good enough to make it on my own.

I had these feelings of fear that I never even knew existed deep down inside. I was this established and successful Executive Director. How could life be taking this unexpected turn? Was I ready to face my new reality? Were my boots big enough to carry the weight? It took me many months, after suppression, depression, suicidal thoughts, and misery, to finally realize my worth.

This is why another job wasn't forthcoming. This is why my resume was being overlooked. God had a greater purpose and plan in store for me. He was ready to use me in a way I wasn't ready for. WOW! It was time for me to push past my real fear - the fear of finding Me. Thank God I stepped out. I never knew who I was until I stepped out afraid.

Let me share A snippet of my story with you.

What God had in store for me, I could not have imagined. I left this place and fell into a deep, dark, state of depression. You know the emotional rollercoaster when you feel like the world is moving on and you're left in the dust. Yes, this was the feeling I had. I started writing letters of suicide. Many would see me and think everything was grand, but they had no idea the hold the enemy had over me. During this time in my life, I took steps to plan my suicide.

This strong and confident leader, felt like a failure. Talking the talk was easy for me, but feeling like a woman of worth, well this was far from my mindset.

Thank God, I reached out to Him. I opened my dusty Bible once again after several close friends sent me links and videos that impacted my life. It was time to pull myself up by the bootstraps. I knew the "woe is me" attitude would never get me anywhere. I'd personally led workshops telling people this for years.

I have always had a passion for helping leaders grow and evolve. Leaders are expected to be ready. They are expected to know the way and teach others to do the same. The underlying fact is leaders are human and will make mistakes. The amount of pressure built leadership roles, if not managed and balanced, leads to depression, health issues, and for some, even death. It is imperative leaders get help. There is a resource and a community that can help them excel while maintaining their sanity as well.

Over the 15 years in leadership, I've counseled and trained many. I've helped them advance to their next level, and showed them how to improve their skillsets and thrive. This being said, I just was not certain that outside of my Corporate America comfortable job that anyone would want to listen to me.

People have often said they saw me doing something bigger. It's so funny how these comments replay in your head years later once you've actually made it to where you're supposed to go. I had to make a decision.

- A decision to love me.
- A decision to realize my worth.
- A decision to showcase my life as an asset.
- A decision to make a difference.
- A decision to step out and make an impact.

I am so grateful I made these decisions. The journey has not been easy. Learning to be an entrepreneur is a mighty feat.

The many letters of gratitude, smiles on leaders faces as they hit their lightbulb moment in our sessions together, and the feedback, all confirm I made the right decision.

I acted through fear and I won through fear.

Jessica L. Thompson
www.mompreneursonfire.org
info@mompreneursonfire.org

Affirmations of Faith

- I have no need to fear because God is with me.
- Anything I set my mind to, I can accomplish with God's help.
- My thoughts, my steps, and my actions are ordered by God.
- Every day is a brand new day full of new possibilities.
- I am a better me because of my experiences.
- My circumstances does not make me. My mindset does.
- I am not called because I am equipped. I am equipped because I am called.
- My heart is in complete alignment with God and I am always in His care.
- The path has already been laid for me, I just need to walk in it.
- The more value I provide, the more value is returned to me.
- I am Royalty and therefore I attract the same.
- I live in expectancy of my God.
- My life is a living testimony of faith.
- I have a story to tell and I will tell it.
- No storm can overturn this boat because Jesus has already calmed the seas.
- My race is for me to run. No one else can run it for me.

- I have light within me and the world needs my light. I will shine.
- I attract strategic partners with whom I can work to build God's Kingdom.
- God's word is part of my daily life. It is planted in my heart.
- People need me. I show up in my purpose authentically.
- I am courageous and go about my mission with boldness.
- I walk in faith because God is on my side.

Testimony – Nikki Ruffin-Smith

Replace Your Self-Doubt, Procrastination and Fear with Positive Words of Affirmation.

I Had to Stop Being My Own Worst Enemy

I realized I was having trouble finding the success I desired because of my negative self-talk. There are many reasons why I chose to sabotage and prevent myself from experiencing success but the main reason was fear. Instead of discussing all of those reasons, I will share with you how I was able to overcome fear to live the life I desired.

I had become stagnant and was not experiencing growth in my business. Red flag alert. I took the necessary time to do something different. As memories of the past began to flood my mind, I had to start seeing them in a different way. Instead of placing blame or being a victim, I identified what I could have been done differently, and the decision to change the way I would normally act.

Give it a Name and Claim the Victory

The first step in conquering my fear was to identify and admit it was the main cause of my defeatist attitude. I didn't want to admit this. However, it was important for me to identify what was blocking my blessings. I have heard it time and time again that if you do not admit to having a problem you cannot get to the solution. I had to get out of my own way. This did not happen overnight. I am not where I want to be. However, I am no longer where I was. I took some time out for self-reflection to identify the negative behaviors. I dissected each situation that led nowhere. I disconnected my emotion, mapping each behavior I identified on paper to figure out my pattern. Once I identified a pattern, I was able to go to the next step.

Replace It by Doing Something New

As with any new habit, you have to replace it with something else. Now that I had named the behavior, it was time to replace it with a healthier option. I flipped the negative self-talk into positive affirmations. I started responding in positive ways instead of reacting in negative ways. I tried doing something new and different over the same old things I had always done. The definition of insanity is doing the same things over again expecting a different result. In the words of one of my favorite Bishops, *"Shake Yourself!"* This is exactly what I did.

I began to ask better questions of myself during each situation. I refused to go back to what I thought was comfortable for me. It wasn't comfortable at all. It was my normal. I pushed past my "normal" and came up with new answers to better questions. No one ever succeeds in life without taking some risks. Now, I am learning to evaluate the risks, and take solid steps toward getting better answers.

Repetition

At first it was quite difficult because I monitored my thoughts like a night watchman. It got easier. It was very important for me to practice. I have heard it takes 21 days to make a habit. It took me longer to replace my fear with faith. I made a few mistakes along the way, still do, but I know in time, I will master this. When I hear the negativity whispering in my ear, I stop each time, name it, claim it, and implement new things.

I have found sometimes I needed help getting to the point of recognizing my negative behavior enough to replace it with better ways. I sought the assistance of a counselor to help me recognize my triggers. The idea of being a better me surpassed any negativity I used to hold on to. I wanted a different path. Within about two months I was a new person, who was out of her own way, accomplishing more than I ever thought possible. Thank God for allowing me to gain the victory.

Nichelle Ruffin-Smith
www.exhaletoexcel.org
exhaletoexcel@gmail.com

I leave you with some additional passages of scripture for you to ponder and meditate on daily, to help you overcome fear, accept God's help and live a courageous life.

Matthew 6:25-34
Therefore I tell you, do not worry about your life, what you will eat or drink; or about your body, what you will wear. Is not life more important...? Look at the birds... your Heavenly Father feeds them. Are you not much more valuable than they? Who of you by worrying can add a single hour to his life? And why do you worry about clothes? See how the lilies of the field grow.... Will he not much more clothe you, O you of little faith?... But seek first his kingdom and his righteousness, and all these things will be given to you as well. Therefore do not worry about tomorrow,

for tomorrow will worry about itself. Each day has enough trouble of its own. (NIV)

Matthew 10:26
Therefore do not fear them. For there is nothing covered that will not be revealed, and hidden that will not be known. (NKJV)

Matthew 11:28-30
Come to me, all you who are weary and burdened, and I will give you rest. Take my yoke upon you and learn from me, for I am gentle and humble in heart, and you will find rest for your souls. For my yoke is easy and my burden is light. (NIV)

Matthew 14:30-31
But when he saw the wind, he was afraid, and beginning to sink he cried out, "Lord, save me." Jesus immediately reached out his hand and took hold of him, saying to him, "O you of little faith, why did you doubt?

Mark 13:11b
Do not worry beforehand about what to say. Just say whatever is given you at the time, for it is not you speaking, but the Holy Spirit. (NIV)

John 14:16-18
I will ask the Father, and he will give you another

Counselor [Comforter, Encourager, Advocate] to be with you forever – the Spirit of truth... You know him, for he lives with you and will be in you. I will not leave you as orphans; I will come to you. (NIV)

Acts 4:13

Now when they saw the boldness of Peter and John, and perceived that they were uneducated, common men, they were astonished. And they recognized that they had been with Jesus.

Romans 8:15

For ye have not received the spirit of bondage again to fear; but ye have received the Spirit of adoption, whereby we cry, Abba, Father. (KJV)

1 Corinthians 16:13

Be on your guard; stand firm in the faith; be men of courage; be strong. (NIV)

2 Corinthians 4:7-11

But we have this treasure in jars of clay to show that this all-surpassing power is from God and not from us. We are hard pressed on every side, but not crushed; perplexed, but not in despair; persecuted, but not abandoned; struck down, but not destroyed. We always carry around in our body the death of Jesus, so that the life of Jesus may also be revealed in our body. For we who are alive are always being *given over to death for Jesus' sake, so that his life may be revealed in our mortal body. (NIV)*

2 Corinthians 12:8-10

Three times I [Paul] pleaded with the Lord to take [the thorn in my flesh] away from me. But he said to me, 'My grace is sufficient for you, for my power is made perfect in weakness.' ...That is why, for Christ's sake, I delight in weaknesses, in insults, in hardships, in persecutions, in difficulties. For when I am weak, then I am strong. (NIV)

Ephesians 6:19

Pray also for me, that whenever I open my mouth, words may be given me so that I will fearlessly make known the mystery of the gospel. (NIV)

Philippians 1:12-14

Now I want you to know, brothers, that what has happened to me has really served to advance the gospel. As a result, it has become clear throughout the whole palace guard and to everyone else that I am in chains for Christ. Because of my chains, most of the brothers in the Lord have been encouraged to speak the word of God more courageously and fearlessly. (NIV)

Philippians 2:12b-13

Continue to work out your salvation with fear and

trembling, for it is God who works in you to will and to act according to his good purpose. (NIV)

Philippians 4:6-7
Do not be anxious about anything, but in everything, by prayer and petition, with thanksgiving, present your requests to God. And the peace of God which transcends all understanding, will guard your hearts and minds in Christ Jesus.

2 Timothy 1:7
For God did not give us a spirit of timidity, but a spirit of power, of love and of self-discipline. (NIV)

Hebrews 13:5-6
For He Himself has said, "I will never leave you nor forsake you." So we may boldly say: "The LORD is my helper; I will not fear. What can man do to me?" (NKJV)

1 Peter 3:13-14
Who is going to harm you if you are eager to do good? But even if you should suffer for what is right, you are blessed. "Do not fear what they fear; do not be frightened." (NIV)

1 Peter 5:7
Cast all your anxiety on him because he cares for you. (NIV)

1 John 4:11, 18
Dear friends, since God so loved us, we also ought to love one another... There is no fear in love. But perfect love drives out fear, because fear has to do with punishment. The one who fears is not made perfect in love. (NIV)

If you have benefited from this book, if your life has been impacted in any way, I would love to hear from you. Send me a note to ranelli.williams@gmail.com or complete the contact section on my website, www.ranelliwilliams.com. Thank you and God bless!

Sources:

1. http://rickwarren.org/devotional/english/god-s-word-is-a-mirror

2. Mays, Steve. *Overcoming: Discover How to Rise Above and Beyond Your Overwhelming Circumstances in Life.* Bethany House Publishers, 2012. Print.

3. www.pathfindersonline.org/pledge-and-law.

4. Douglass, Herbert E. *Messenger of the Lord: The Prophetic Ministry of Ellen G. White,* Chapter 11. Pacific Press Publishing Association; First Edition, 1998. Print.

ABOUT THE AUTHOR

Ranelli Williams is passionate about helping individuals overcome their fears and activate their faith to walk in their purpose. Known as the Faith & Legacy Building Catalyst, she empowers small business owners to master their personal & business finances and embrace the idea of building a financial legacy for future generations.

Ranelli is an author, speaker, and entrepreneur. She is the Founder of The Legacy Builders Network. In addition, she is Co-Founder with her husband, Eric Williams, of ERJ Services, LLC, a tax and financial consulting business.

She graduated from Borough of Manhattan Community College with an Associate's Degree in Business Management; and from Baruch College with a Bachelor's Degree in Accounting and a Master's of Business Administration (MBA). Ranelli is a Certified Public Accountant (CPA) and is currently pursuing a Doctor of Business Administration Degree in Entrepreneurship at Walden University and has embraced Walden's adage in being an agent of social change.

Ranelli started her career in Corporate Accounting, then spent a few years in Public Accounting performing external audits for non-profit organizations, and finally transitioned to working for a Prescription Benefit Manager as an Internal Auditor and Project Manager until leaving Corporate America and taking on full-time entrepreneurship. Ranelli has also worked with the National Association of Black Accountants, where she served as Chair of the Employment Committee and worked with the Financial Empowerment Committee. She has coordinated and presented at various other financial workshops. She was also a member of Toastmasters where she held multiple leadership roles including Club President and Vice President of Education, and she has earned the distinguished award of Competent Communicator. Most recently, Ranelli has partnered with SCORE to share her expertise with local entrepreneurs and help contribute to their success.

In her church ministries, she has served as Youth Leader and Mentor, Youth Sponsor, Assistant Treasurer, Assistant Stewardship Director, Assistant Choir Director, and as part of the Education Committee.

From an early age, Ranelli has not only been a lover of higher education and learning, but entrepreneurship has also been her passion and because of her love for Christ recognized the importance of marrying God and business. After becoming Dr. Ranelli Williams, her hope is to further expand her entrepreneurial pursuits by establishing an organization to help individuals transition into entrepreneurship and become strong leaders for God's kingdom. She endeavors to do this through teachings, workshops, and one-on-one mentoring.

Ranelli and her husband live in East Stroudsburg, PA, with their sons, Joeraan and Jaevaan.

Connect with Ranelli:
Website: www.ranelliwilliams.com
Facebook: www.facebook.com/releasingthefear

**Take the
Releasing the Fear & Walking in Faith
Challenge**
visit www.releasingthefear.com for details